CANTO y GRITO
MI LIBERACIÓN

RICARDO SÁNCHEZ was born in El Chuco (El Paso), Texas, and raised in El Barrio del Diablo (The Devil's Ward). He has been director of several programs dealing with Chicanos: he has published extensively in periodicals such as the *Afro-American, El Grito, Carbunkle Review-Magazín,* and *Nosotros.* Poet, writer, consultant, and lecturer, he has also spoken at universities throughout the United States on topics ranging from Chicano culture to sensitivity programs to the Movement.

MANUEL G. ACOSTA was born in Chihuahua, Mexico, and grew up in El Paso, Texas. He had art training at the Chovinard Art Institute in Los Angeles. His work has been exhibited widely throughout the southwest United States.

A Chicano

CANTO y GRITO MI LIBERACIÓN.

(y lloro mis desmadrazgos . . .)

PENSAMIENTOS, GRITOS,
ANGUSTIAS, ORGULLOS,
PENUMBRAS POÉTICAS,
ENSAYOS, HISTORIETAS,
HECHIZOS ALMALES DEL
SON DE MI EXISTENCIA . . .

by Ricardo Sánchez

ILLUSTRATED BY
MANUEL G. ACOSTA

ANCHOR BOOKS
Anchor Press/Doubleday & Company, Inc.
Garden City, New York

Canto y Grito Mi Liberación was published in a hardbound edition in 1971 by Míctla Publications, Inc., El Paso, Texas. The Anchor Books edition is published by arrangement with Míctla Publications, Inc.

ANCHOR BOOKS EDITION: 1973

ISBN: 0-385-06864-6
LIBRARY OF CONGRESS CATALOG CARD NUMBER 72-89676

This book is the first in a series to be published by Míctla Publications . . . it is the birth of an idea first gestated in the frenzy of Soledad Prison ten years ago, and now becoming a bronze reality.

El Paso, with all its memories, remains the cauldron of chicanismo for me; thus now I return via my writings to my brithplace to explode out expletives and cantos . . .

This book would not be possible were it not for the patience and understanding (and typing help) I've received from my wife . . . needless to say, it would likewise not be possible to have it published were it also not for Raymond Gardea, M.D., who has been un carnal a todo dar.

This outpouring is dedicated, como toda mi vida,

>   a Teresa,
>   Rik-Ser,
>   Libertad-Yvonne,

to the memory of mi jefe, Pedro L. Sánchez,
>   mis carnales Pete y Sefy,

to the love felt from mi madrecita, Lina,

to Mannie, Luy, Katy, Mary, Rosie, Helen,

>   reymundo gardea, lalo, narciso,
>   manuel acosta, tony parra, cha cha,
>   eduardo, cleofas, rojas felix,
>   willie camacho,

>   al migrante del campo,
>   al bato del barrio,

>   to mis suegros—manuel y estela—

to all of you, and all those others whom time and space keep me from accolading, i extend this verbalized set of esperanzas escritas, experiencias gritadas . . .

cariños,

RICARDO SÁNCHEZ

Nov. 11, 1970—año del Chicano
Sept. 11, 1971—año de carnalismo
>   *birth of Mictla*

TABLE OF CONTENTS

SOL DE ORO BRUÑIDO

En este nuevo amanecer
el Chicano se levanta
con ganas de estirarse
y fuerza pa' toser

Pulsan en sus venas
grandes fuerzas
de conquistar,
soñar,
querer . . .

Le ilumina un sol ardiente
que le tuesta hasta la frente,
dando dimenciones a su sombra
a la que el Chicano nombra
la medida de su ser

¿Por qué tan lejano y majestuoso
este sol que lo vió nacer?
por qué, si calienta tantos seres
¿le desprecia su querer?

Te va a conquistar—verás,
o sol de oro-bruñido,
aúnque quemes como diablo
este Chicano te cojerá dormido

Manuel G. Acosta
2-23-71

ONE YEAR AFTER:
reflections on/about/around the Movimiento. . . .
A PREFACE (of sorts)

"No hagan las gallinas reir," an old saying about not making the chickens laugh, yet, still and all, a saying that typifies much of what passes for involvement, not only in El Paso—that dusty, sun-backed pachuco city—but also in the bustling and hustling metropoli of Aztlán, i.e., L.A., Denver, San Anto, etc. The cackle is heard loudly, boisterously, and things continue on their not so merry course, day after day, month after month, millennium after millennium.

A year ago, I was hectically pursuing the impossible—so it seemed—course of trying to set up Míctla Publications in El Paso, while at the same time getting our first book together. Many were the questions, doubts, and reservations expressed—by whites, blacks, and Chicanos. Though there were concern and enthusiasm on the part of a lot of carnales, there was also the feeling that I would fail—and sometimes that I *should* fail.

In order to begin organizing Míctla, I had to leave my position with the Colorado Migrant Council (as director of the Itinerant Migrant Health Project) and start the ball rolling. Prior to coming back to El Paso, I met with people from the Interracial Council on Books for Children, and through their contacts I was able to write a short, cryptic article on the need for Chicano and minority publishing. *Publishers Weekly* ran the article on the following week (March 15th, 1971, issue), and this served as a strong impetus for our coming to the attention of the public. The response to what we were projecting was fantastic, but at that time I was Míctla, for I had not yet met the people who would give structure to the embroiling ideas running through my mind.

We—wife, family, & self—packed our things and began the trip back to El Paso, to that city repleto de barrios y duelos. My wife was joyful, I could read alegría dancing in her eyes; my son, a rapidly expanding boy, exuberantly talked of Turi (his friend), his grandparents, and other things on the way; my daughter merely gurgled, unconcerned, for her world was still a reaching out with nine-month-old fingers to a world full of mysteries; and myself? Damn, but my thoughts went to family and

11

carnales I had not seen in quite a spell, and I literally wanted to shout out all the liberating ideas/feelings I had gathered from throughout the country.

The abruptness of meeting up with El Paso and the realization that things hadn't really changed was psychologically disorienting—for a pinto (ex-convict or convict) is merely an exotic piece for discussion, as long as he keeps his distance. I became aware that I should have stayed away; for many quasi-movement types felt uneasy and challenged by my presence. There I was—hablando y gritando y cantando about "let's set up a Chicano publishing house," and there they were, keeping their distance. Some told me bluntly that they felt I was not of the right persuasion, and (this was hilarious) even asked if I was from the barrio. Others, like a fellow who supposedly was one of THE LEADERS, smiled politely, and then walked away to call me names behind my back. It was about this time that I heard that a would-be carnal was going the rounds talking about my being with the man/placa, but some batos who had done time with me in the prisons of califa y tejas laughed their heads off. Not surprisingly, he has never confronted me about his suspicions. I wish he would!

During those first hectic, turbulent weeks, I had the good fortune of meeting some dedicated young carnales and carnalas. Some were from the different barrios, and others were with MECHA, MAYA, SHAMROCKS/BROWN BERETS, etc. I also came into contact with older batos who were extremely aware and sensitized—though I did not know of their commitment. All the while, I relied on those carnales I had known before, and all the while things were turning against me.

About this time, José Antonio Parra and Patricia R. Sutton approached me and asked if they could help with Míctla . . . it was because of their dedication and fervor that much of what is Míctla exists. Along the way, we came into contact with a young, highly motivated and very intelligent man—Eduardo R. Ochoa. A coalition of sorts came into being and the process for the incorporation of Míctla came into focus. Our primary goal was to get out and see that *Canto y Grito Mi Liberación* was published, for through the erroneous reasoning of a would-be friend, the book had been contracted out to the wrong printer. By working with such friends as we really had, namely John (JOHN Q.) Siquieros, Dr. Raymond Gardea, Manuel G. Acosta, Ralph Aguirre (and his lovely wife, Lydia), Joe Medina, Bert Hernandez, Antonio "Cha-cha" Marín, Rogelio Felix, Noni Tenorio, Gera

Araujo, El Monchis, and too many others to mention, we finally did our thing.

In the span of the past year, I learned—or re-learned—the significance of the words: CANTO Y GRITO MI LIBERACIÓN. No longer was this phrase only signifying an existential process wherein man must voice his liberation, but rather it became an arduous set of experiences whereby it meant being told in word and adamant deed that in order to survive I WOULD HAVE TO CONFORM ... conform to the wishes of a parole officer, who demanded utter capitulation, otherwise my parole would be revoked in no uncertain terms, and this because it was—AND IS—my contention that man must be a free agent and act for the good of humanity, and if this meant confrontation, so be it. It also meant that I might have to go back to a Tejas prison (for eight years), and I was naturally scared, but one's reality is that one must sometimes pay in order to play, and my wanting to serve La Causa was stronger than my fear of La Pinta. He, as usual, could not and would not accept my being involved in the movement—and he went so far as to restrict my travel for a time, thus I could not go on lecture/speaking tours, and this became an economic hardship, for I had neither a job nor a way to make it in the business community—for who wants to hire an ex-con? Fortunately, a carnal in New Mexico heard of my plight and he hired me as a consultant, and I must admit that a manito—Tomás Atencio— is largely responsible for my having been able to retain much of my sanity. After much hassling from this parole officer—and in turn hassling him through the intervention of carnales committed to justice—he got off my case. At this writing, there is another parole officer, and he does not seem to want to hassle me, but as always in the life of a pinto, my fingers are crossed and my mental/emotional world abounds with hopes that this new p.o. will not be arbitrary, for in the final analysis (and not parenthetically so!), a pinto is powerless, has neither civil nor political rights. I have been able to maneuver enough to do those things that I must as a bato in search of a morality that goes beyond the superficiality of un mundo tecnológico y mentiroso, but ever with a flighty sense of hope, wondering when this moment or that shall become another ordeal, another senseless expenditure of time and energy.

Other—and more serious—demands for conformity came not from the readily recognizable establishment, but from a neo-oligarquía—the poverty pimps in charge of most (95% or so) federally funded programs.

Now these pendejos are the dangerous ones, for they have lulled the community and co-opted the movement (to them it is movidas, not movimiento, ¡y que si las mueven!), and they will not hesitate to destroy if it means their newly acquired status and high salaries (color them pastel-brownie and very much self-aggrandizing coconuts). This group has it down pat . . . they have even adopted an almost barrio patois which they use very emotionally when they rappingly weep out about what it feels to be desmadrado (deracinated), and they laugh on their way to the bank. Middle-class mentalities and escuardas-de-a-madre (square, non-bato loco, clean-cut types), weekend revolutionaries and 8 to 5 chingones del movimiento, the new elitists. It appears that being Chicano has become a lucrative credential—especially if one has the other loftier credentials also. And some Americans of Spanish surname (A.S.S.) do in fact have all kinds of credentials, i.e., ex-parole and ex-probation officers who used to put down the bato loco (but who now profess to love them); welfare workers who proclaim their love for the barrio poor (when before they were cold, calculating types who abhorred poor people); pretty boy sports types (who were all-american high schoolers and never questioned their teachers), and others who see money in their becoming more *barrio-istic* and *bato-loco* than los desmadrados. . . . The movement has become a chiaroscuro kind of vaguery, for the enemy is no longer easily definable; he now also looks like us, dresses like us, talks like us, and thus can do more irreparable damage to us.

Being articulate and having some expertise in programs and organizing, I filed application after application with Project BRAVO, University of Tejas (El Paso) Chicano projects, and numerous other allegedly movement-oriented agencies, organizations, etc. ALL TO NO AVAIL! Through countless interviews I came to find out that the poverty pimps will not allow articulate carnales the opportunity to *serve* La Raza. "Ricardo is too articulate and he rocks too many boats," was a common complaint. Yes, I was too qualified—a bato who was a high school dropout, ex-convict, and could run circles around the bureaucrats. Bull shit! The punks had won one more round.

That was bad enough—but not enough to discourage me or the small group who wanted to set up Míctla—strong people like Dr. Gardea, Tony Parra, Eduardo Ochoa, Patricia Roybal Sutton, John Q., and others. Yet, it was not the fact that no one would jeopardize either funding or the program by hiring a pinto like me (one who has to ever be protesting and talking too much about morality and justicia) that hurt—No! It was knowing that all the while somebody (or some-bodies) had been telling the man (parole authorities/police) just what, where, how, and when I was doing anti-establishment things. Some-times the stool-pigeoning (relajando) was undue, for much of my time was spent on Míctla or in grubbing for a measly $50 consultantship from agencies in need of legitimacy in order to feed my family. Still, those people who made it their business to supply the man with in-formation that would destroy me continue on, getting funds with which to further destroy the people—and all this in the name of the people.

Why this book? In answer to the anomie, hurt, destruction of a people, etc. More so in response to the growing menace of a de-humanizing society that is now worldwide, for conflict and racism are rampant throughout the world. The awesomeness of the world and all its resources belong to all the people of the world, and *Canto y Grito* is my way of saying that we must all stand still for a moment and realize how morally irresponsible *man* has been . . . we must declare our humanity in very unequivocable terms. This book then is about a concrete, deeply realized affirmation of self—it is about that monstrous feeling in the gut lining del alma that demands to be heard and dealt with on a humistic level: I ADAMANTLY SING AND SHOUT MY LIBERATION! In the face of uptight amerika, in the face of racism, in the face of moral cowards, I staunchly proclaim my right to my own humanity—and it is beautiful—gratifyingly beauti-ful—to sense how much of a threat a man can be only because he wants to realize as much of his humanity as possible. Thus, this is my song of love for the valleys, mountains, cities, plazas, women, children, carnales, carnalas, gentes, and entirety of the earth; it is also my anger at our failing to create a society of caring, our failing to attain human-ness . . . for the spoils of Attica abound, just this moment I heard that a couple of carnales from the Black Berets in upstate New Mexico were wantonly and brutally murdered . . . it is thus an indictment mixed with a hopeful plea that the unsanity of this manmade idiocy be righted—for our morality demands it, for our humanity commands it, for without a change in course we are damned all the way to hell. My son, beautiful child, quizzical child, chess-playing child, trusting child, even now asks why the disparity between the different amerikas. Let then no child sleep, half-naked on the international bridge linking juárez & el paso, at three in the morning, huddling in the cold—and his hunger showing through ribs, and his empty eyes questioning a world bent on marginal profits, while much of humanity lives desecratedly on the vaguest of societal fringes . . . it is against the madness of those who want to become masters and despots that I fling out my angers, for totalitarianism abounds . . . it is to La Causa, to universal man, to cosmicity, to the merging and mutuality of all human beings that I sing love songs, it is to that growling, caressing sense of life that I write out what it means to me to be human, to be liberated, to create worlds wherein my spirit walks assured of itself. It is more than hope, it is making each moment count—that my relationships might be meaningful, that in turn the flighty and scanty moments of my existence might not have been in vain.

It is to the whimsical (on the surface) craziness of Tony who is business manager and spiritual director and mystical carnal at Míctla Publications; it is to the turbulent screeches and sense of life of Eduardo Ochoa; it is to the deep sense of huapango-type human-ness of Dr. Gardea when he lovingly accepts all humanity; it is to those who share my madness, my angustia, my frequent outbursts, and my flipping realities that this means so much to; it is likewise to Chuck & Pat; and it is that sense of barrio and pinta life that keep churning and burning, deamadre, but it is in the main good to live as if background music accompanies one at most turns. Let us then clean up the world and create vinculum and avenue for the exploration of the grandest of human traits: cultural, ethnic, and racial diversity—for it is our differences intertwining that will create humanity . . . look not to blending or smelting down processes, for life is pungent, spicy, and multi-flavored . . . it is also balanced—and we must never cease struggling, for it is the struggle that makes the human experience worthy. Let us struggle together that we might all be worthier . . . for wisdom dictates this . . . if we fail to find meaningful areas of commonality, then we shall doom ourselves and turn to hate and total destruction. It shall be through sharing that we will create a moral world—mutuality is the key. It shall be through people telling it like it is and has been—not for your pity nor for hand-outs, but that you might become aware of your human/moral responsibility, that all the rhetoric of euphony, equality, and brotherhood might come to pass . . . that no longer will there be masters and slaves, for both live in a world lacking dignity and human validity . . . one for oppressing, the other for not defending himself . . .

vi la lluvia anoche, amor mío,

sentí el duelo
y nos separamos;
hoy te busco
en los callejones
de mi mente/alma
and i find a shadow
lurking
where we last kissed . . .

sadly, knowingly
we went our ways
and still
memory lingers,
sticking
to la fíbra de mi ser . . .

vi la lluvia anoche, cariño,

te admití
a las avenidas de mi existir;
you accepted
and in a lusty, total sense
love became us . . .

life is woman,
but it is more
it is mankind loving
without reason,
just because love
must exist . . .
it is mankind defending
all and parts . . . it is being aware
we all exist.

Viva La Causa

Ricardo Sánchez

INTRODUCTION:

Little notice by other than Chicano writers and poets was paid to the emergence of the first Chicano literary quarterly, *El Grito: A Journal of Contemporary Mexican American Thought,* in 1967. Needless to say, the Quinto Sol writers of *El Grito* were leading the way for what has since come to be known as "the Chicano Renaissance." And Chicano literary production since 1967 has indeed been a renaissance in every sense of the word.

In the great Renaissance of the Western World following what historians blithely call "the dark ages," the reborn and rekindled spirit of western man sought out the great verities of life in the words of bygone ages. But more importantly, there followed a creative surge to expand the revitalized awareness of the word by writing new dramas, new fictions, new proses, and new poetries. For a renaissance illuminates one's vision of his surroundings and of his future in terms of what he finds relevant in the past.

So, too, the Chicano Renaissance has expanded the revitalized awareness of Chicano writers beyond the peripheries of what most Americans accept as "the American experience." Chicano writers are challenging the truth of the American word. For the American experience has been a fiction perpetuated by the dominant Anglo American society at the exclusion of the realities of American life. In other words, the American experience came to be what Anglo America thought it was. This is part of the message in *Canto y Grito.* And controlling, of course, the public media, Anglo America foisted on all "Americans" the Anglo American way of life, rooted in the Puritan and Cavalier tradition of the Atlantic seaboard. In most cases, in only one generation the children of immigrants became thoroughly Americanized—"assimilated" has been the word for it. The "melting pot" concept was so successful that after a generation Americans whose forebears came from other than Anglo stock had so internalized the Anglo myth of America that they identified more with the Anglo tradition than with the tradition of their forebears. Considering that American education was predominantly in the hands of Anglo Americans, it is little wonder that in the space of a generation the children

19

of immigrants were indoctrinated to the American way of life.

But "assimilation" worked only with "white" immigrants. "Colored Americans" were rejected by the assimilation process, though many of them had become Anglo in all but the color of their skins. "Integration" also failed because the concept left most "colored" Americans at the margins of Anglo society. The legal fiction of equality worked fine in the public domain save for the sector of social intercourse, the most vital pressure point. And, again, race was at the root of the failure of integration.

"Cultural pluralism" has emerged as a concept for curing the racial ills of American society, but it too operates from the point of view of the dominant culture. In the United States this is, of course, the Anglo culture. And as long as the American experience is defined from the perspective of the dominant culture, there is little likelihood that "cultural pluralism" will succeed. For "cultural pluralism" depends upon the wisdom and magnanimity of the dominant group, a wisdom and magnanimity which has been conspicuously absent from Anglo America judged in terms of its record with American Indians, Blacks, and Mexican Americans.

The only alternative is "cultureity," where AMERICAN Indians, Blacks, and Mexican Americans "up" the Anglo society and create their own viable alternatives for existence, without approval of the dominant society. This is the hardest road of all, but it appears there is little choice for non-white Americans. For we have reached the last racial frontier in the United States. The test of our survival as a nation depends upon whether we can overcome our racial prejudices and biases. The democracy we espouse must be more than symbols scratched upon a carefully guarded parchment; we must practice what we preach, otherwise there will surely be an Armageddon of the races.

And so Chicano writers are writing new dramas, new fictions, new proses, and new poetries. The Chicano writer has a vision for a better way of life. And perhaps, as the Chicano poet, Abelardo Delgado, put it, Chicanos may yet be the salvation of American society.

Frankly, it is the Chicano poet who most articulates this salvation. For the Chicano poet, like poets from other ethnic groups, articulates his vision of life with unparalleled clarity and force. One need look only at the Greek poet, Homer, or the British poet, Milton, or the French poet, Baudelaire, and many others to see that the poet is a special kind of human being. Unfortunately, though, the poetic vision of a better life is oftentimes a radical departure from the realities of controlled existence. For a poet advocates the ultimate freedom: to be. And humankind has ever been wary of freedom. This is why, no doubt, Plato thought to bar the poet from his utopian Republic.

One cannot help lament the visions of Ricardo Sánchez, for as a Chicano poet he has endured the hardships of his race. His every word is ladened with the travails imposed upon Chicanos by an insensitive and unresponsive Anglo society more concerned with the profit from Chicano labor than with compassion and care for their survival. Ricardo speaks of "all humanity/but an eternal convict/suffering the binding of its soul." His words cut across the tissue of hypocrisy like the surgeon's double-edged scalpel parting swiftly and surely the preliminary layers of flesh enroute to the disease. More often than not, Ricardo expresses only the grim vision of existence in Anglo America. But one detects in his poetry and prose a decided optimism when he is talking about the strength of Chicano carnalísmo, the kind of brotherhood that creates respect and dignity for the worth of the individual though we may be of different persuasions. One cannot help but conclude, as one reads *Canto y Grito,* that only one who has suffered the whips and scorns of life could emerge with so much concern for his fellow man. For Ricardo is speaking in *propria persona* not to just Chicanos but to all of us. His voice, like the voice in the whirlwind, beseeches us all to redeem our humanity lest we perish by the ravages of the animal instinct confronting our spiritual essence.

No contemporary poet reminds me more of William Blake than Ricardo Sánchez. I do not mean in form or style, for Ricardo is a Chicano poet through and through. No. I mean in purpose. Like Blake in his time, Ricardo Sánchez is trying to tell us something. I only hope more of us stop and listen.

Philip D. Ortego
El Paso, Texas

21

THIS IS (MI COMPA) SÁNCHEZ

It is harder to introduce a compadre than one of the best exponents of the chicano word. A couple of months ago, at the Guardian Angel Church in East El Paso, Lola, my wife, and I had the honor to make a christian soldier out of Libertad-Yvonne Gurulé Silva y Sánchez. Let me approach it this way. Most of us upon seeing an automobile accident, a fist fight, or if we are males the "puerta" shown as a woman or young girl sits coquettishly showing her curvy wares, our natural instinct is to get a closer look, either by situating ourselves closer, wiping our glasses or simply getting closer. So with the chicano movement and with the chicano himself, our whole lives merit a closer look. It is in the writings of Sánchez that one can afford a front seat, nay, a microscopic view of the alma chicana.

Sánchez is no exception to great writers having their yo-yo moods, and if one is lucky and close enough to him, one may catch an inspired original Sánchez poem written on a napkin as one sips draught beer. It is at times as if the muse was his very shadow, and he could reach out any time or place and grab the shadowy inspiration and convert it into neat explosive verses.

Watching Ricardo walk and talk and just be himself is poetry in itself for the man can, as he puts it, go through changes from the innocent perplexity of a boy growing up in a gringo dominated society, to the pachuco "conectando" in the alley, the young man exploring Juárez congales, the young man eating wise words of wise writers in wise books, the moody prisoner blending in the *gris* of prison and now the husband, father, fighter of lost migrant causes and a variety of other moods passing like neon colors through a neon sign.

These moods can only be captured into words by the possessor and such are his writings containing an inner fidelity which facilitates expression. Many men are paradoxes in that they possess noble, holy brilliant thoughts, but are unable to express them either in spoken or written word. Others, through some discipline, capture in entirety the art of expression both in oratory and journalistic endeavors, but have little to say of themselves and rely on reproducing someone else's great ideas; such is not the case with Sánchez. He has something to say—and the ability to say it.

It must be a very sad existence to live in a constant state of pregnancy with ideas of how our world should be, pictures of how beautiful it is to be chicano, quejas of how it is to survive the tonelada of social pressures strange and foreign and coarse . . . it must be sad, uh, compa?

Abelardo B. Delgado

3 de Octubre, 1970
el valle mágico/trágico
Pharr-Tejas
Aztlán

Opened letter to my conscience

Conscience:

Lo, verily have I ever questioned my own development and sense of self; seldom have I taken myself to task when failing to follow-through on those aspects of my life that need redemption . . .

Now—here, this very cauldron of chicanísmo—I stand confronted by the paradoxical qualities of el valle de tejas . . . a tragic, yet magic, valley teeming with the desmadrázgo y belleza de la gente de bronce. On every hand there is the dominant force of racism trying to oblivate la raza, while in every hovel there is the force of chicanísmo . . . just driving thru McAllen, Pharr, Edinburg, etc., the soothing madness of need seeking the answer takes on a balming effect, and my soul soars high—higher than even grifa could take it. And I am forced by the legacy of Jacinto Treviño, José Angel, and countless other carnales who have told the angry, bitter, racist gringo world to hang it up, to now strive to not only better understand myself, but to become so involved with my people that only a new social order can stem the tide, only a new social order can begin to mete out the justice that we not only need, but demand. The pride in our people is a real, tangible thing . . . it can be measured in the looks of love shared by friends, lovers, and relatives throughout Aztlán. It is a reality articulated by two chicanos meeting on the street for the first time and extending their hands, saying simply, "mi casa es su casa," and meaning it.

This then is my redemption—the writing of this book in the hope of sharing it with family, friends, and raza. To my wife, without whose understanding and support, I would not have been able to survive the horrendousness of prison life in "la tejana" (the ramsey prison farm in texas); to my son (Rik-Ser), a light in my most darkened and turbulent years; to my daughter (Libertad-Yvonne), a liberating spirit challenging me to become a more meaningful person with each gurgle that she utters; to my mother, a woman of strength and love; to my father, now deceased, a man so strong that he could cry and express his love for family in the most virile/masculine way possible; to my parents-in-laws, two of the most giving people I know; to Lalo Delgado, a wise fat man with the soul of Quixote de la Mancha, Santo Tomás de Aquinas, and the average chicaspatas riding on the crest of his honesty; to the pent-up mad cabrones y desmadrados doing time (behind bars or on the streets, for we all are slaves somehow); to the migrant with all his cultural beauty and strength and his empty belly; to the city chicano now plotting a return to dignity; and finally to a carnal with an M. D., a man who cries out soulful anguish amidst the reality of economic power, a man trying desperately to express his human reality, a man who is rapidly becoming so real that he is starting to terrify his world—to el mero doctorcito, Reymundo Gardea del pachuco, tejas.

Here, then, my compadres, carnales, y familia, is the residue and moment of truth and half-truth that I write . . .

26

Soledad . . . .

When a man goes to prison, he becomes an integral part of it; and it, in turn, is unto that man like a big protective womb. He might try to rebel against the security afforded him by being good and getting out soon because he knows deep down that the more he accepts and adjusts, the more of a robot he will become. If he succeeds, chances are that he will never be back in prison again. If he fails, he will shortly give up his garrulous rebellion and become institutionalized and will eventually die in prison. The poem that follows is neither about a rebellion nor a submission; it is about the sheer feeling of aloneness that is ever gestating in prison, and ever is this feeling seeking a means of aborting or expressing itself. I wrote SOLEDAD on the 29th of November, 1961, a week after I had been told by the Adult Authority Board of the California Department of Corrections that I would have to spend another year in prison—conform, they whispered. That year has elapsed, and it is now like having spent a lonely eternity in the throes of torment and anguish, for I knew not which way to turn or go. The name of the prison is Correctional Training Facility, North at Soledad, California. It has been three years now since I was first arrested. . . . I get out of prison in seven months . . . three years of being a vagabond hindered from meandering into the limitless pages of his own personal hell and/or heaven. The title of this poem is Soledad, but November 23, 1962 or 6:30 a.m. watching the bulls make count or cell 341 in b section of Lassen Hall or whatever else could serve just as well for a title . . . Soledad means solitude in Spanish, to me it means differing levels of interminable deaths. . . .

soledad . . .
               my soul bleats
lonely, lonely, lonely . . .

a night—some time ago,
long ago—Los Panchos
sang of
          women of perdition
and love . . .

my soul cried!

Two, three or five years . . .
doesn't matter.
So long ago
love went.

Remember her smile,
and the way
she . . . ?
well, do you?
what for?
she'd hate this . . .
too concrete.

smelted steel, toilet-grey
                colored labyrinths;
soledad
inundated with turmoil,
and my identity's lost . . .
only instant coffee matters,
tobacco, god, and tobacco.
rosh hashanah, chanukah
and ave marias,
intercourse of the hand
and ominous square pyramids
where god
            nurses guns, guns,
and more guns.

nasty wires . . . barbed & piqued;
fences—so celestially high
one can't return, run,
        o,
mi barrio/chicano,
my other life
show me,
tell me
        once more
of my peasant origin;
give me a happy, canorous

grito . . .

damn,
make these chains break!

soledad,
you lied!
    no solitude or serenity here,
just tormented souls . . . no,
not souls.
    o   please   unsanity   go   back!
only your mountains matter,
your name is wrong,
your keys clang at midnight,
your phantoms stalk, search,
and
haunt . . .

      I smoke my pipe,

          I drink hot tea or coffee

            without

              sugar

              or

                cream . . . .

soledad,
your austere vacuousness
gave me
    look-alike de-animated death;

two words, yours, guard me:

          hell   &   dreams.

soledad,
god made li'l birds weaklins,
    murdered flies at midnight,
and
you killed me for a cup of vengeance.

soledad,
i saw you first
            through the myriad of misty eyes,
through condemnation,
through lonely vigilance
            as i plotted
        a hasty-never-to-come-escape.
you received me
like you've received your isolation, &

tomorrow will be like today, why?
there is no future,
hope   died
in the ovens . . . desecrated
because god (cops?) did not smile!

soledad,
land of retribution,
nation of rough guys,
            toughs and male whores,
owners of syphilitic brains
            shuffling by aimlersly:

we—they—are the cool cats . . .
            ha . . . ha . . . ha . . . ha . . .
            god must've laughed
    (for)
            nothing matters,
all is a shuck, lie, sham,
                thoughtlessness!

soledad,
    so dead,
    so soggy . . .
                    abuser, mis-user,

soledad . . . .

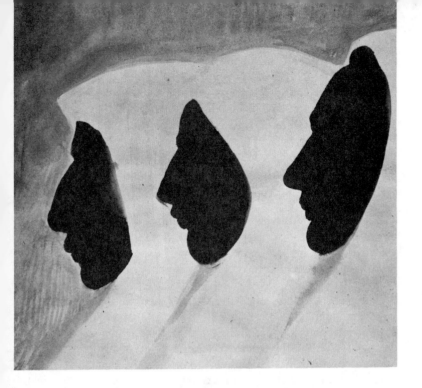

Desmadrazgo

Chicano needs for self-determination have been tumultously pro-
pounded by would-be ideologists and sociologically oriented saviours
during the past fifty years, yet their ramblings have failed to cast a
true, meaningful look at what it is that the Chicano wants, what the
Chicano manifests with his every act and word. The latest in a long
series of self-proclaimed Chicano experts to study the Chicano is Stan
Steiner, who, I feel, crucifies his subjects rather than suffer the stings
of arrows himself. Steiner's myopic study of La Raza is more farcical
than factual; more projection than observation, and more in keeping
with the bland image of the gringo of himself than with the recording
of the virile machismo and hembra-ismo of La Raza.

Stan Steiner and all self-proclaimed experts on minorities should
go and study the weird habits of the gringo—from the heinous perversity of Manhattan (where people are plastic) to the sordidness of
the South; from the infested sores and hunger of Appalachia to the
mafiosi hideousness of Chicago; and from the putrid avariciousness

of the Texas Tragic Valley to the sophisticated hypocrisy of California . . . therein lie the fertile fields of fermented racism of the gringo for them to study! There and nowhere else.

From the placid valleys that they describe—in reality, valles repletos de orgullo y desmadrazgo—to the urban settings they depict, there survive a people with enough spirit to have been able to thwart the genocidic mania of Amerika.

What is this mass of brown people? Who are they? Where do they come from? What are their goals, objectives, and reasons for seeking a change in the status quo they have been forced into?

The Chicano is a product of linguistic and cultural dichotomies—Mexicanism, with its fervor, spiciness, piquancy, and humanistic sense of life, and the desmadrazgo of being forced to live under the oppressiveness of the anglo-amerikan system of exploitation. Granted that not all things amerikan are of an exploitative nature—just most of them.

The desolate Southwest, with its sage, cacti, and serene beauty, is largely populated by the Chicano. As to who the Chicano is, he is español merging with naturaleza indígena—a composite of passion, compassion, cariño, and human-ness. A pride of being, family, and comradeship becomes a dominant force, and the human dynamic of never forgetting, slighting, nor exploiting one's people takes on the disciplined philosophy of La Raza Cósmica. This sense of self (machismo for the man and hembra-ismo for the woman) takes on the trappings of a beautiful daily life experience—affirmation and confirmation of one's existential reality. Thus Chicanos hold their heads high and proclaim their right to dignity and human decency. This sense of human-hood has been the victim of u.s. suppression, and it is mainly an unvoiced protest/indictment against this alien culture (the gringo system) that Chicanos continue speaking their own language. What is unrealistically considered the amerikan way of life is basically an alien form of cretinism to the Chicano—for how can these foreigners be American, when the Chicano has antecedents in these lands (the Americas) that precede the gringo and his systematized racism by at least 12,000 years.

A people who had once walked this land proudly and with dignity were made to feel less than human by the invaders. The Chicano—whose name comes from Meshicano, the original name of the Aztecs (the spaniard heard about these Indians coming from Aztlán, so he called them Aztecas)—has traditionally been on the receiving end of the exploitative, racist, and imperialistic debauchers of the world. First the gachupín and later the gringo. About the only difference between the gachupín and gringo is that the gringo would never think of merging with different peoples, an hispano/indio confluence—both culturally and physically.

The latest invaders of Aztlán, in their racist onslaughts on the Chicano, managed to dispossess the Chicano. Chicano lands became gringolandia. Under the force of gun and whip. Chicano labor built up the huge agricultural combines of the Southwest for the foreign invader with the blue eyes and quick, silvery tongues that promised much and delivered neo-colonism and slavery.

My people—La Raza Cósmica y Chicana—were thus re-enslaved. It was but another conundraic moment of servitude imposed by the many despots that the Chicano would come to know by many a different name—español, gringo, sistema, etc. At this moment, with all its rhetoric of freedom and mothered-up sentiments of would-be democratic life, now—today—in the 20th Century, Chicanos are still slaving and feeling the brunt and whip of this mad-dog society. Peonage is a reality in much of the migrant stream; disenfranchisement is a tautology in the barrios; and hatred against Chicanos is one of the stronger forces running rampant from one point of Amerika to the other.

Amidst the hurly-burly clowning of national figureheads—paint them white and exploitative—come statistics attesting that Chicanos earned their rightful place in society during the war (WW II), and they also go so far as to say that out of that war came many Chicanos who took advantage of Amerika's goodies by enrolling in colleges under the G. I. Bill of Rights. True, some Chicanos earned degrees; some even wrote treatises; and others were given highly paid window dressing government jobs. What is precisely true is that all of them only got menial tasks to perform. These (not even vendidos, for no one cared enough to buy them, but regalados, for they gave themselves cheaply to a system only interested in Judas Sheep) did the bidding of society. They returned to set up the G. I. Forum, Good Americans Organization, LULACS, etc. Under these bogus terms came about the impetus for social justice. Returning combat heroes (during and after the 2nd World War) demanded a change of venue. Carnales who had the huevos (courage) to amass the highest concentration of National Medals of Honor awarded to any ethic/racial group (same holds for Korea and maybe Viet Nam), now ate up the resonant rhetoric of their having earned their rights. By blood and gore, they had striven to prove themselves Americans. Amerika, by default and fraud, had proven itself unyielding to the clarion calls for justice—and Amerika proceeded to further enslave, through the jargon of assimilation and integration, a people who had their own culture and language.

For such a long time we had been duped—duped that we had to earn essential human rights. We who had walked this land before there was a Columbus—walked these lands 10,000 years before Christ walked in Galilee. Some of us came back from that miserable war—Guadalcanal had our blood on its beachheads, so did Europe. Some of us were not willing to turn tail nor be relegated to stooging out lackey errands at the whim and call of the gringo hierarchy. Some of us, with medals in our pockets, were killed for wanting service in cafes and restaurants—from Denver to L. A. to el Valle Mágico. Some of us, combat trained and aggravated beyond recall, went back into the barrios, into the turbulent mass movement of the Pachuco.

America was not willing—nor prepared—to receive the Chicano. And the Chicano not being too articulate, not yet being a politicized organizer, and not having avenues for meaningful confrontation, asserted his machismo in the garments of el bato loco (hipster): zoot-suits, ducktailed haircut, khaki pants, french toed shoes, switchblade, chains, and caló (the language of the barrio). These formed his fighting and all around uniform. The rejecter came about—the kind of Chicano who wound up telling Amerika to go to hell. He was more than merely dispossessed—he was, in short, totally disgusted with Amerika and wanted no part of it. His motto was not "separated on the streets and integrated between the sheets." He was not out to barter his soul for a new car.

Thus the Pachuco became a movement—a movement that had its genesis in El Paso, Texas. A city that would become known among the carnales as El Chuco (the pachuco city). The Pachuco movement went back many years—to the 1930's in the streets of el Segundo Barrio. It took the war years and heightened hysteria in Amerika for the pachuco to become known. These were the first Chicanos in large numbers to become dedicated to fighting back, dedicated to protecting the community at all costs. These batos locos, with crosses tattooed on their hands, had a deep sense of respect and love for their families.

In his low-riding uniform, he cruised the streets—not asking, but demanding and taking what rightfully belonged to him. Though it was not an organized thing, Pachuco groupings popped up everywhere.

Every city or hamlet where Chicanos make up part of the population had its clique. Even songs were written about them—Pachuco Hop, La Pachuquilla, etc.

In east el chuco, there by the El Paso Coliseum was an old barrio—El Barrio Del Diablo. Here lived the batos from the X-9 gang. Batos sworn to protect the barrio from gringos. During my youth, I never saw gringos walk through that barrio. It was not until the mass media and the police destroyed us that gringos were able to walk those streets. They destroyed us by lying to our people—by convincing the older Chicanos that pachucos were just a bunch of hop-heads who blasted pot and cooked little children. Vicious portraits were painted of us. Not all gringos hated us—for a lot of them copied us (hairstyles, stomper gangs, etc.), the only difference being that we were trying to keep all gringos out of our lands.

The horrors of the Amerikan dream and the awesomeness of racist reality forced the Chicano to seek escape. Drug cultism became an avenue for blotting out the dream—that vicious dream with its multi-headed dis-realities. There were no ideologists or ideationists then to structure out a revolutionary thought pattern or to educate the people. La Raza had only the emotional outbursts of Pachuco spirit to guide it. The danger of drugs, and their subsequent circumvention of the need for a new society, was not taken into account. The Pachuco gave birth (on a large scale) to the Chicano civil rights movement. Regrettably, this mass social protest was aborted, for frustration, hunger, oppression, racism, imperialism, et al, were neither intellectualized by the community nor explained. Society first sought to ignore Pachucos by disregarding the plight of the Chicano masses. Finding that Pachuco activity was disrupting Southwestern economy, the power elite (gringos) had all its resources structure out a campaign to disparage, destroy, and annihilate Pachuquismo before it could influence more Chicanos.

Police officials (los perros) and gentlemen (?) from the Amerikan Press called the Pachucos a menace, a disgrace, hoodlum, criminal, vicious, and horrible offshoot of La Raza. Older Chicanos (striving for acceptance from the gringo) believed in their minds what their hearts rejected, and they too turned against the bato loco. Chicanitos were made to feel even more ashamed of being not only Chicanos, but Pachucos. More and more, repression in the Southwest took on the Hitlerian garments of racist, genocidic madness.

Lack of organizational skills forced the Pachuco to go underground during the late 50's. Submerged, he lay—thinking, plotting, and soaking up organizational skills. The plight of La Raza had to be alleviated, somehow . . . and soon!

Education for the Chicano was, and continues to be, a farce. The Amerikan education system has methodically endeavored to destroy the sense of culture and Chicanismo of La Raza. Courses have been oriented solely to the gringo and his whims—thus we find that all school courses come under the label of White Studies. Never have Chicanos been taken into consideration, other than when vocational courses in plumbing, street cleaning, etc., have been in the planning stage or when school districts are about to ask the federal government for more money.

Schools throughout the Chicano Southwest have traditionally punished children for speaking Spanish on the school grounds, unless the child happens to be white, then said child is commended for being precocious. The punishment meted out basically consists of swats, scoldings, or staying after class to write "I WILL NOT SPEAK FILTHY SPANISH" 500 or more times.

A system that hates naturally tanned, other language speaking people, yet preoccupies itself with becoming tanned (via bottles of bronzing emulsions) and strives to learn Spanish, French, etc., is a very sick system. It is a system that bewilders people whose only interest has been to live and let live, to love, share and help.

The disparity between material hedonism and the puritan ethic has caused the Chicano to view society with horror. Not wanting to compete in racing toward total or partial de-humanization, the Chicano has dropped out oftentimes. Society, in not leaving the Chicano alone, has oftentimes forced the Chicano to lash out with blade and anguish. In spite of our constantly telling this damn nation to back off and let us be, we are consistently harrassed and maltreated. Our homes are broken into by cops; our brothers are shot down in bars; our people are brutalized; and even those Chicanos with skills and power are abused (witness the assassination of Rubén Salazar). There will be no Watts for us, but rather a succession of Kern Place in El Paso, River Oaks in Houston, Wilshire and Beverly Hills in L. A., Nob Hill in San Francisco, the Heights in Albuquerque, etc. 140 years of confronting this society has left us with sensitivity to the vitriol of this genocidically manic nation. Our chests now swell with anger, and every gringo—CADA UNO DE ESOS PINCHES GRINGOS—is a target. There can be no escape for anyone for his/her culpability. Just as all Germans are responsible for the frenzied idiocy of Hitler and the Nazis, so are all gringos in Amerika responsible and guilty for the debauching of La Raza! There is no way for them to cop out, they are indicted once and for all in the reality of history.

Discontent, lethargy, hate, turbulent twinges of revenge, a driving energy to fire at the world, a million drives and furies: these make up the new zoot suit of the revolutionary. Thinking has jelled. Now there is structure and organization. The ancient cry of the Meshica (Ni Tlaca—Aztlán/I too am human—my bronze lands) has taken on a new lustre. The Brown Berets, MAYO, MAYA, MAPA, CRUSADE FOR JUSTICE, and other organizations have started on the road to taking reparations and following through with planned out strategies.

The Chicano, in the main, never did—and still does not—want assimilation; there is no sexualized compulsion for making love to a blue-eyed, blonde gringa. The Chicano has ever been calling for that which is his by rights—moral rights. Ours is indeed a question of morality versus the anti-human stance of the Nixons of the world and all their jive about law and order. Their laws and their orders—things which legalize the persecution and manic genocide of the peoples of the world. WE DEMAND THE RIGHT TO DIGNITY, THE MANI-FESTATION OF DIGNITY IN ALL THAT WE DO; WE DEMAND AND SHALL TAKE THE POWER TO DETERMINE OUR OWN DESTINIES AT WHATEVER THE COST; WE DEMAND FREE-DOM!

All the citadels of the Bronze People—El Paso, San Anto, Denver, Alburque, Los, Tierra Amarilla (where Tijerina attacked and fired a meaningful salvo for the freedom of La Raza)—have become haunted by the spectre of Chicano voices angrily demanding, and Chicano actions bringing about revolución. We no longer ask—now we take, and shall continue taking our reparations.

No longer will La Raza allow itself to be exploited. The Del Rio, Texas, Manifesto to the Nation demanded freedom and justice for the Chicano. Denver's Crusade for Justice came out with the "Plan Espiritual de Aztlán," a declaration informing the world that Aztlán belongs to the people, that Chicanos are sovereign. The creation of Colegio Jacinto Treviño in the Valle is but a step toward the fulfillment of our liberation. We shall create our own Chicano society—y si no le gusta al gringo, pues—¡que el bofo chingue su madre y en abonos pa'que le duela!

There is talk of a 3rd world coalition. Such a coalition is an important factor in the coming changes that shall transform Amerika's barbarity-and-people-chewing into a just society built on love, trust, freedom, justice, and truth—all of which must be weighed humanistically.

Chicanos are now realizing that there is nothing to lose for they have nothing, so therefore there is everything to be gained. That is why more and more Chicanos are prepared to fight, regardless of the consequences, in order to change this heinous social structure that makes slaves and things out of humankind.

Machistic chicanismo with its strong sense of carnalismo has been resurrected. There is more than wishful thinking in our minds and flighty misty hope in our hearts. We have the beauty of our self-awareness (and he who does not love himself does not in fact love anyone else!) which affirms our bronze humanity. We, los mestizos del mundo tercero, are aware that we are not alone in our struggle against the desmadrazgo of the Useless States of Amerika. We affirm that justice, dignity, freedom, and human-ness are more than worth fighting for—they are the main reasons for being. We realize that (like our old carnales pachucos) we must prepare to fight our war here in the barrios, campos, y valles—not in Asia. This then is where we shall either bring about change or die fighting for an ideal—an ideal worthy of Cuauhtemoc's blood, Zapata's soul, and the trials and tribulations of La Raza. We must, and shall, do away with el desmadrazgo de ésta sociedad (o—¿es suciedad?) tan cruel . . .

> bronze is beautiful
> y al demonio con el gringo,
> ser chicano es vivir
> realidades como humano
>
> ser gavacho es vender
> alma y cuerpo por dinero,
> consumido por racismo
> el gavacho es gringo seco . . .

un canto por la naturaleza chicana y que viva la hermandad, que viva la humanidad . . . viva la revolución!.

EL AÑO CHICANO!

and it . . .

carnales,

cuando en el curso   del desafío y desmadre
it becomes imperative to pick up estoque and filero
          crying out the anguish of mi alma;

when, you bastards of the jive language,
it all becomes unbearable
to live duelo y pésame y desmadrazgo

and feel   the lancings
of unsane social madness
and continue
          ad infinitum
                    under lasting latigazos

feeling hurt of a million years,
hunger of a thoughtless epoch
          carrying mind to old virginny lies,
sepulchred in u.s.a. proverbial mendacity
midst genocide and hatred,

y mis huevos hinchados
bulging
con la angustia
          de mi hermandad desnuda . . .

i awaken
in the cauldron of reality,
hands stretching out
to garrote   hydra-headed racism,

caught
cataclysmically
in analytical tonterías . . .

product of noria
gone dry como el río bravo
cerca de el paso,
where children starve

while dancing
to the master's hateful tune;

—and it hurts, and it hurts, andithurts
    hasta que mi misma casta
                  GRITA
    a ringing obscenity even more obscene!—
        (even ernie ham-the-buey
          would shrivel in his tomb
          while viewing la pobreza
            in the southwest!!!!!!).

chicanitos born only to die   swollen eyes and bellies
    in the land of plenty   and it hurts, and it hurts,
                and . . . .

We were lost . . .

It came about naturally enough: we wrote out the dismal truth in our most hurting moment. I had been seeking reality, so I thought, when catastrophe hit me right on the face. We were lost, and we had to face it—that is if we gave a goody-goddamn about surviving. There we were, right in the middle of Texas, near Dallas, in fact, and we were stranded.

It wasn't that we were broke—hell, we had all kinds of money. Nor was it that we had no transportation, for we were driving a new Fury III, and brother, it was loaded down with all kinds of options. The real fact of the matter was—and still is—that we were lost. All at once we realized that there existed no one in this world that we wished to communicate with.

We had become so disgusted with racist jingoism (and that is not rhetoric, friend, but reality), that we had decided to drop out. Well, we dropped out—but unfortunately, society and its phoneyness are beyond us; so pervasive is the societal way of life, that there is no place for anyone to drop out to. Even to find a place beyond the social structure we had to go to a social establishment for a map. We had seen a service station a few blocks back; we backed up, and I told the man to fill up our tank and check the oil. I also asked him for maps—maps of the state, the country, and Mexico. He got me the maps, then he proceeded to attend to my other mechanical needs. Meanwhile, we perused the maps. We studied them from every angle possible. Every place, we soon realized, was but part and parcel of society—irrespective of any choice we made. We stood there angry, hating society with every pore of our beings (we were very well synchronized and calibrated).

"Shall we try the mountains," my mate asked. Her eyes were quizzical and mystic like; her voice quavered a bit; and her stance responded to the resonance of her voice.

"No, not the mountains, for they usually swarm with hunters," I remarked. Meanwhile my mind traversed other moments when she had asked other pleading questions, and I seriously entertained the thought of . . .

41

We debated as many alternatives as came to our minds. Nothing seemed right. Just when I had made up my mind to write the final stroke to my rejection of the system, a harsh voice broke through the patterns of my thoughts. "That will be $6.50. Cash or charge?"

I hurriedly dug out my wallet, silently handed the attendant a credit card, and unseeingly waited in my car to sign the chit. I signed for the gas, drove out of the station, and resigned myself to being lost for the rest of my life.

Reo Eterno

reo   reo   reo   reo
como un canto feo
del pasado

the loneliness life is
caught in the mesmerizing words
you are now sentenced
to die day by day
in the sordid world
of cement and bars . . .
the endless shuffle
of prison garbed demons
and the hated banging, clanging
of prison guard keys

and corky rapped of
being "lost in the swirl
of a gringo world"

y los reos protestan
el chingaderismo
dentro
those leaden labyrinths
where the soul dries as it dies
and love is a four letter word
cauterizing plastic celluloid dreams
and playboy fold-outs
and muted memories that haunt
a sleep that knows no sanctuary.

out in the streets
z movie announces the loss;
it is a variation
of the same thematic desmadre—

all humanity
but an eternal convict
suffering the binding of its soul;

43

and the gavels come down hard,
hard nosed justices mete out
measured eternities

from capitol hill to wall street jungle
and humanity doesn't have a chance . . .

and no one seems to give a damn . . .

Tap, Tap, Tap

tap, tap, tap . . .
again do your heels tap;
their resonance
                    echoing,
                    reverberating
from wall to wall,
mockingly manifesting
your inner savagery . . . .

rap   rap   rappity rap . . .
fiery fingers
manipulating castanets,
madly proclaiming
                    your artistry!

your just born in the jungle eyes
betray your wanton-ness!
yes,
glide
     away
swiftly,

let your audience
                    go home,
o,
so hungry,
desperately desiring you . . .

you're being betrayed,
though,
BY YOUR EYES . . .
eyes, without comparison,
eyes that tell,
nay, that shout
your secret loathing . . .
for the multitudes!

sadly it is,
your tomorrows
          shall have less flowers
than your yesterdays . . .

like all women,
you were born to die
and
dying shall leave you:
               desiccated,
devoid of soul

               too soon!

Evening in Prison: Theme & Variated Vibrations—
Beethoven's Quartet in C Sharp Minor/Strings

amid crescendoes or conviviality,
betwixt softness and strains of peace,
        inaugurable tintinnabulations lilt out
        muted love calls from my famine/weak esprit . . .

it is a night of pure remembrance
hailed by the euphony of strings—
        & i can only mentally galavant
        to other star-struck nights
when you were the all-engulfing warmth
and your pulse the beat,
        your words the structured melody
        and your rhapsodic sighs
the finale to our own composition;

Dearest, someday
        we shall again hear
        Beethoven and
we shall be enraptured;
our love shall keep time
        to strings at evening hues and
        burst forth crescendoes . . .

Beloved, conciertos and love toasts
enlace us, bind us;
        we are en-webbed cocoon/like
        in the caressing wool music/love is . . .

Virtuosos—rabin & horowitz—lull out
symphonic overtures
        that haloize you,
        and lovingly
do i see you palpitate
depth and totality

　　　　　　　with love's musicality
　　　　　　　complementing you . . .

tonight soft sounds shall emanate
and flood my thought world,
　　　　　again i shall behold you
　　　　　in the furtiveness of hope . . .

Something or other

chicano feelings, knowing that,
and feeling that all is not well . . .

going to sun plaza
seeing happy anglo oldsters
enjoying
things foreign to chicanos
        (because chicanos are dark,
           because things
                of value aren't meant
           for us: so we rebel and
              you can't understand it!).

what, if anything, must we do
to prove that we too are worthy?

must we prove
that we are more american
(which we are!) and
that therefore
we need not suffer?

o, foolish majority,

there is no need
for us to prove our humanity . . .

i think it is you
who is doubtful of your own human-ness,
not us . . .

we fear not treating others with basic human dignity . . .
yet, you quake at the thought
that others might prove to be more human
and dignified . . .

51

anglo-america,
you do i pity
        for the patheticness
of your wretched souls (assuming
                    you are capable of
                having such things as souls).

**Thoughts While Sipping Coffee at City Hall
Cafeteria in Company of One Jaime Puertones
(Jim Gates to Y'all!) During Info-gathering
Jag for the Mexican-American Committee on
Honor, Opportunity, & Service/MACHOS, For Real.**

soft strains, hispanic mood,
court house shop
     and it's all un-real.

dark-grey-suited representative
eye averting
        (possibly can't or won't
           keep campaign pledge);
coffee a la government,
yet, bureaucracy foliates
and sterility abounds

thoughts go un-gestated
in the fat gut womb,
and the government burgeons . . .

while sandal-footed individualists
make notes
on the last
     (I hope)
dying
   gasp
     of
       regimented idiocy!

In Exile:
The Only Chicano Outpost in the Olde Commonwealth
Of This Here Virginny . . .
Thoughts/Poems . . .

Sojourns in Virginny . . . .

June, 69 to January, 70

it is by way of definition that i
now write this short introduction of myself,
                    a chicano,
lost in the wilderness of the deep south, and
very perplexed am i about this place . . .

my thoughts go back
        to east & south el paso, texas,
a brown speckled, non-honey-dripping
sort of place
where i grew up
in the welter of texas ranger hates
and idiocies . . .
to be a chicano in the state of texas
is likened to being black or jew
or you-name-it in any auschwitz type of place:
        not an ideal place for a sojourn . . .

my life reeks
of the hates
inculcated in me by
a blind, yellow-haired, blue-eyed,
de-humanizing culture . . .
my chicano blood
        boils
and i strive only to express myself
in order to determine my own course . . .
and this then is my aloneness,
my being confronted by a vacuum
and

i write of my people—LA RAZA!—
with pride, love, and out of need . . . for
    i am indelibly CHICANO.

    to justice, freedom, and humanism . . .
                                    ¡viva la causa!

Flight: San Antonio, Houston, Atlanta, Richmond
From El Paso . . . . .

Hedonism reigns
and simple
poverty-worker status
obsoletes ideology . . .

year's worth, mi Raza,
and
surcease to old turmoils
appears possible,
yet,
El Paso brown/faced hunger
                    haunts me

and

I question
      self-motives
and
one year journalistic fellowship
relegates La Raza, causa, etc.,
to minor role
      (if only temporarily)
and
mi alma weeps out
        its paradox;

pathos—theatrical soul/masks
laughing, crying—
family
discord according,
airport café mélange . . .
friends, la causa makers
cauterizing instantaneously
      multiple lacerations
and more . . .

mine cicatrix
         decorated soul/mind
recapitulates

     and
          then accepts
the test . . .
               hurt . . .

and i
am lost
in maelstroms

San Anto

citadel of La Raza,
missionary's goal site,
place
    where continental jet
blows tire,
and
  we placidly await
  time consuming tire change;

san anto
home lo' these many epochs
    to chicano heights and
              grim lows;

two chicano soldiers (u.s.army)
got off
after extending
    LA RAZA UNIDA SALUTE
and handshake;

two chicano army/batos
destined for homeleave
followed
    by war's
        destitution
          in a rice paddy

instead of a bean field
    where they belong;

how much longer, san anto—
        you haughty home
of el bato loco—will you
and El Paso/Los Angeles
    be bastions
  of chicano humility

a
la subservience
                syndrome?

                        lo pobre es
                        invivible
                        todavía

6/19/69

Dr. Gardea: Compatriota . . .

you've travelled far,
                    old man
           in the snappy stance of youth,
and
el chicanismo is your chant now . . .

Manuel Acosta's portrait
of brown-power coalescing
        with black-power
captivates your inner demon force,

and

you wrestle
seeking
        ego/id rapport

and
    sanity;

do not ask of me
    balm
            and/or
                    condiments

or soul indices;

we both exist
                for no reason
                        other than being . . .

yes,
you too innovate

on thematic strictures
for a deitical idiocy

and

find there is only life—
    so you live . . . .

                        sus duelos,
                        mi raza,
                        son míos . . .

This of Being the Soul/Voice for My Own Conscienceness Is Too Much (Petersburg, Virginny)

MARCH, CHANT
scream out need
and misery;
hope against hope
that long, cold wintry precipitations
lead not
          to long, hot summers—
hope and strive
to heat up society's icy innards
that we might all be humanized
real soon . . .

Today, Petersburg & Richmond,
I saw girls—
young, fragile, and wise—
sing out with human strength
and valor
the wisdom(s) of the afflicted
and brutalized . . . .

Bearded, weirdly clothed leaders
remonstrated and denounced—
so, that "god is not dead
          but three black children are!"

much hurt
and even now the stirring musication
"we shall not be moved"
tintinnabulates
          in my soul/stream;

now—yes—now
is the time to raise our voices
in protest,
for justice to come
to all our people
          (brown, black, yellow, and red)

that we might not
slash out, brothers, and
spill more blood needlessly;
but then
i say
that even if blood must be spilled
that we might all
achieve human-ness,
spill it now
while the young are
        salvageable,
not tomorrow when
            we've all gone . . . .

O Seré o No

time has genuflected its
prescribed idiocies
     to me   for the last time

and beers drunk
in southern tavern

talks on mexican-american
       quandaries
and césar chávez
huelga buttons . . .

and somehow it seems
weird
that
california affects
      virgin(ia)
in-as-much

   as
there is word
that 14 brown berets
          were busted

for looking at reagan (the governor)
cross-eyedly
and
starting a riot/fire

and the charge
is attempted murder of a pig
in the guise of governor

and the world keeps turning

so that a mad-cap chicano
can protest stupid
         caricatures

of taco-juice-drippers
being humble
before   the master . . .

madre, todo
is too much, and my soul
boils its juices and
        i shout
YA BASTA!   to uncomprehending fools

and hope

that it is not too late . . . .

Two big thighs . . .

2 big thighs . . .
one brown, one black,
engulf
      and swallow up
             resolve . . .

little white children look on

and

envidiousness swims
nakedly in their eyes,
asking the assuaging caress
            dark thighs are . . .

Juárez, El Paso, Richmond

the mind spits out
carnivorous idiocies
        and
rejection comes about
after involvement.

what is more primordial
than the lightless madness
of this commonwealth nightmare
so devoid of cuneiformic truth?

let darkened hungers
lip out a final dirge . . .
      that lingual attenuation
    cease

and the well run dry . . .

Nobody really understands . . . anyway.

Lo Humano . . .

free university discursiveness
and
bearded, chirping neo-christs
roam streets;

social salivations

demean
uncombed, miniskirted women
unjustly;

love a la humanism
escorting mad innerbeing
to
resorts of the mind

and
thoughts
of making it
to paradisical rendezvous
to be
    only to be
the
   quixotic equation
             one is meant to be;

why does it startle
          you

to feel a strange hand
caressingly appreciate
           the totality you are,

and to hear
spanish words
that
   tell you

the pleasure you can be?

has your basic human-ness
been
    relegated to clandestine meeting places
by the harshness
your environment has always been?

Thought to a million experiences culled from my youth . . .

>   nomás hoy existe,
>   mujer,
>   nomás hoy
>
>   en lo humano
>   en lo chicano
>   en lo existencial
>
>   in search
>   of dignity
>   and human-ness
>   and love
>
>   man trips over himself
>   finding
>   that his today is known to him
>   and seeks
>   phantasmagoric tomorrows
>   hoping
>   that their shimmer is greener
>
>   y el hombre muere
>   secamente desmadrado
>
>   youth cannot be recalled
>   by the wishy-washy sentiments
>   of turbulent tossing/turning at night
>
>   dreams
>   cannot abort
>   today's reality,
>   for
>   today must be lived
>   and its tumultous bounce
>   must be loved . . .
>
>   only today
>   can matter
>
>   for now is when I live . . .

Stream . . .

Middle america . . . middle ameriKa . . . it all is the same
when hate becomes the calling card and out of stream
consciousness, out of migrant stream patterns, the same
crappy situation evolves time after time, and everything is run together like crazy quilt pattern, and
people live, die, and somehow nothing is ever resolved
in their lifetime . . . and does it—or anything—ever
come to matter . . . somewhere, now, a child is dying
for lack of certain things, and no one seems to give a
damn—other than the child's parents, and they are
helpless parents, while society or what passes for the
elite ruling class attends groovy party and nice,
rounded fanny gets pinched and broad married to one
fat-cat winds up in hay with her husband's friend, but
her hubby won't mind, for they both can share his
friend in as many different combinations as are
possible—for this is amerika, land of pubic liberty
as long as you don't get caught, and nothing is truly
immoral, except being poor and/or helpless . . . so that
immoral child and its parents better get on the ball
and learn the name of the game and how to play it . . .

> y duelos leídos
> en sermones religiosos
> son paradojas
> señalando
> sonidos huecos,
> tres bíblias
> cambiadas por los terrenos
> del afamado rancho king
> bajo los resos inútiles
> de sacerdotes ciegos y racistas
> acama los enfermos
> mientras aclaramos
> cuestiones vanas

                    creo en un dios verdadero
                    cerca del basudero,
                    ahí en el atascadero,
                    un solo dios verdadero—
                    la gente en el humidero,
                    un solo dios verdadero . . .

          y los rinches
          como casi-dioses
          y alcabo el dios
          amerikano es racista,
          borracho y pirújo,
          una pantalla
          con cara de pallaso
          y alma de baboso,
                              aún lo cuentan
                              los gavachos
                              un solo dios verdadero,
                              el barrio un quemadero,
                              la muerte ya mero-mero,
                              un solo dios verdadero.

and the subway ride continues on from lexington avenue
to becoming the el in bronx by 125th and the night air
chills the body, while 5th avenue satiny broads pro-
menade ailing aimlessly in their loneliness . . . nearby
in massachusetts with its many empty universities, more
desecrated assaults on the spirit is the name of the game
around fireside chatter about bahai folklore and wishful
thinking, conversion of ex-militant blacks . . . a new toy
for middle amerika, this of persian religious order and
ritualistic rhetoric of brotherhood as long as niggers
remember that their place is near enough to hear them
but not to touch them, except during humanistic education
workshops (purely experimental to see if their kinks
are springy and their smell pungent with musk and gringos
turn up their noses even then), and that goes for all
minority people . . . and a porty-rican (un borícua de manhattan), quien se llama johnny cabrón, he believes he
has white brethren . . . and they'll smite him and they'll
smite him, til he learns that he's not white . . .

oda de fé soñosa
miel amarga

crujía sepultosa
cautivadora del alma

un grito por mi hombresa
gemiendo bajo la presa

verdad que grité en mi sueño,
la busca un borinqueño

oda de triste verano
dentro el desmadre chicano

el existir pa'la raza
es duelo que en vida pasa.

and his sugra-(like nigra)-dripping illusions of nirvana
cum míctla via panacea become the mandible spewed out
honey madness of racist resin in amerika—and he, like
other confundidos, dies a man without a soul . . . it is sad
that there exist those who in trying to sell themselves
have found no one to buy them and they can only become
regalados . . . their souls cast away in hope of acceptance,
and never are they accepted . . . gift horses looked in the
mouth by a system bent on cruel oppression, repression,
and human suppression . . . and some fight for medals for
decorum, only to lose their sanity in the end and wind
up in v.a. hospitals, hopped up, loaded to the gills on
nembutal and stimulants, cruising labyrinths and empty
rooms, their souls hanging limply . . . eyes hollow and
lusting, mind plotting, and inside an insidious need for
self-affirmation.

el vacío derrama
la voz angustiosa
del alma; es mejor
vivir o morir como hombre
que besarle los huevos
al boss/rinche,
ese pinche desgraciado.

i phantasmagorize about the stream of my life, wending
its way—como un duelo penumbroso y al mismo tiempo como
canto ilustroso—from the madness of east el paso
pachuquísmo en el barrio del diablo, out there by the
coliseum—between hammett and boone streets, from paisano
drive south to el río grande . . . and i ran streets in the
anguished futility of a chavalón encabronado y encojonado,
with a yearning itch in my hands for a filero to use
against the hated unknown force(s) that seemed to control us through school systems geared to disparage us,
shopping areas designed to make us hunger for that which
we could not afford; and time passed and i grew up with
anger and confusion reigning side by side in my being . . .
one moment, jefferson high seemed the avenue for my
salvation, until racist teachers (mcbride, willis, travis
& co.) and vendidos (i.e., mares, mendoza, & peña, inc.)
turned me off, while beguiling (or trying to) the carnales
to pursue a materialistic, roboticized life (si, you
young kids can get those new cars & fancy duds, etc., just
by bartering your souls to mad-eee-son-of-a-bitch-avenue!).
i was youth at the crossroads without a map or turn signal.
the army finished the job begun by the schools; i became
flame of need for mine liberation—and i vented my furious
desperation with gun and madness, that monstrous bitch
residing in the gut lining of my soul/mind . . . and sunny
california gave me from one to 25 years in prison, and i
mulled over and over in my mind, between el desmadrazgo,
eviscerations, the canards handed me by a bigotted/unsane
society; the cloister of soledad prison steadfastly
demanded my capitulation; i could only retreat into a
world of dreams and hopes—while reality assailed me to
conform   conform   CONFORM!   and all about me i saw
humanity deform itself . . . years passed in the space of a
hope born, nurtured, and then wantonly killed. eternity
became the blinking of my eyes, and i stepped out of
prison with turmoil defining the drive in my soul . . .

> the chirping of birds,
> even that is cold-blooded;
>
> two years
> and you sent me four letters;

            the steel of the bars,
            cement of the floor,

            stripes sear my soul,
            cold sttriiiips my being . . .

            la pinta is death,
            day by day you pay out,

            the price is your sanity,
            the hurt is reality,

            escape from rejection
            leads one to nowhere,

            the chirping of birds,
            even that is cold-blooded . . .

streets of el paso, you received me with frigidity and
indifference. i no longer had youthful trust. my life
was turbulent—the see/saw machinations of hunger/lust
stemming from deprived ansiedad de la pinta . . . pinto viejo at age 22, as if mockery were to instigate a coup-etat
sobre mi vida . . . came out breathing decadence and hope,
weird merger, paradoxical and wanting change for the
better (i had read and believed all the jive bullshit
about rehabilitation that prisons are notorious for
disseminating) . . . lonely, hurting, needing, and my mind
kept churning out razones filosóficas a través de mi
existencia—and i continued being el pobre de ricardo's
kind of sartre, camús, platón, et al—while sensing the
perversity of juárez nights, sojourns midst el gran
putísmo . . . y yo gritaba aún sin saber profundamente el
por qué de mi vivir tal como vivía dentro tiniebla, como
refugiado de la anciosa absurdidad. noches i spent
enloqueciéndome momento por momento dentro el putísmo
de la calle mariscál—de club a club . . . hasta que llegue
a conocer muchas putas por nombre, and i was numb with
despair—and in my now numb anomie i sought nothing,
yet anger and angustia assailed me until i ran from the
putísmo into the purefying arms of a woman who gave me
her nourishing love and purity of spirit and being . . . a
woman both sensuous and real, one who could uplift my
soul while enflaming my visceral body and we became

an earthy fusing of body and emotion . . . we wed and even
then it all seemed confusing, this of fusing, when all
about us the world was topsy-turvy, universal scurvy . . .
Teresa, esposa, you with trust in heart, hope in your
bosom, passion in the way we kissed and embraced, yet
a way of life that had never known other than the shelter
of your parents' home, i came rampagingly into your life
with a million angers and a will to either change society
or destroy it, and you visibly trembled at the strange,
strong way i assailed an unyeilding world, and you stood
by me . . . i frightened you, yet our love se enfloreció, &
our son, Rik-Ser, came into being. Teresa, i watched
anxiously the swelling of you with our son, and i never
realized that i would come to know him only after he
was four years old, for once more i went to prison—two
days before his birth, i stood alone in my mind indicted
for robbery, you meanwhile suffering the pangs of birth
deliverance, also alone . . . aloneness, the condemnation
of humanity—aloneness! robbery committed in anxiety
and desperation; joblessness so i pulled jobs—and you
both waited while i spent tumultous years pent up in
texas—ramsey prison farm no. 1—years of quasi-college
courses at alvin jr. college, working first in the fields
picking white gold, later in education department, ever
striving to jive the man to grant me a parole, and my
jive worked, for i got out . . . only to find i still was
imprisoned within the horrendousness of a social structure
predicated on stricture and desecration . . . but i got out
march of 1969, this time more dedicated and devoted to
transform the gelatinous globulin of society . . . and el paso
again stood on my horizon . . .

> horizonte paseño,
> duelo de juventud,
> calles corridas
> hambrientamente,
> mi alma un peñasco
> mi vida un poéma

el chuco, ciudad furiosa
nacimiento del chicanismo,
cuna del carnalismo,
creadora ciudad de llanto
        de medianoche

el paso, conocistes mi tristesa
mi locura y mi desmadrazgo,
corrí tus calles y callejones
gritando ansiedad y buscando liberación;

volví a encontrar amor
en los besos apasionados,
en los brazos cautivadores,
en los ojos como norias de cariño
de mi amada y querida señora, Teresa . . .
Teresa, hembra complementando
mi hombreduría,
somos fuego y rigor,
amor y lumbre estética,
somos existencia,
somos paradoja,
somos lo que somos,
y seremos
el vuelo
de nuestra propia trayectoria;

hijo,
hechizo de amor y enloquecimiento,
de la experiencia chicana,
del aprecio vidal que vivimos;
Rik, fíbra de mi ser y
extención de tu madre, mi esposa,
eres
llanto del alma
y grito de alegría . . .

rik   rik   rik
    como el timbál sonando
    y la canción gemiendo . . .
la realidad

                    se desarrolla
                    cuando la vida es valerosa . . .

              rik   hijo
                         te
                           quiero . . .

el paso streets . . . the southside, VISTA M.M.P. work and
MACHOS, where i rapped about liberation and in between
words, i wrote out past and present, knowing that tomorrow is a finite concept ending with the sunset . . . and
never had i had a sunset . . . other than the closing of all
doors, so it seemed, and being sum and total of social
brutalization (i am chicano!), sheer idiocy gnawed at
me . . . demanding that i rip off a world belonging to my
people, but controlled by middle ameriKa. nights that
ate out my innards became days that dazed me with the
cruelty of too much light—light that burnt and cauterized,
congealing the hurts in my soul. el paso, you insatiable
bastard thing, cold and unrelenting, conniver and deli-
berate obfuscator, era miseria otra vez hasta que cha cha
gardea, y otros carnales destendieron las manos con apoyo
y ayuda—and my stream elongated and expanded . . . from the
mired-up madness of amerika's hateful south (virginny)
to washington, d.c., baltimore, new york, and massachusetts . . .
then on to chicago, harvard, yale, northwestern, columbia,
etc., all for rapping and more and awareness . . . then to
denver, oregon, michigan, the mid-west, and on and on . . .
and i lived in the jungle of lalo's pad, mi compa abelardo
a fat-gut chicano who lurks in my unconscious like a
neo-buddhist cristo, wonder of wonders, the martyr of
south el paso, bato/carnal, there in denver with the
colorado migrant council co-directing itinerant health
program with juan coyotero gilll-eeesss-pie, el mucho
malo kid when it comes to coyote killing on king ranch
grounds enroute to the valle from houston . . . denver, abject
city of chicanos who no longer pueden hablar nuestro idioma
(mestizaje), y les digo, carnales, que duele al oír mi
raza periquiár en inglés o que éllos pidan poesía chicana
escrita en el idioma del gringo . . . y no puedo traducir
ciertas cosas, pues siento mi alma brotar cantos del

                          81

espiritu chicano . . . y mi ser demanda la verdad de nuestro
carnalismo escrita con sangre apasionada . . .

>   denver   denver   denver
> en el lanno* rojo
> de enojo
> en colorado
> con cruzada por la justicia,
> donde carnales
> como corky, gurulé,
> ken luján, narciso,
> y especialmente
> abelardo (que no es) delgado brotan;
> lugar del ya natalizando chicanismo
> donde gorilas ávila y tigre cantan
>
> oficina del concilio pa' migrantes,
> calle grant numero 665,
>
> denver, ft. lupton, alamosa,
> pueblo, springs, las ánimas,
> tienen parte de mi alma
>
> t. rotole con señal de paz,
> tu que eras sacerdote,
> hoy buscas paz en mis palabras
> y hallas el pésame hecho del desmadre,
>   tal ha sido mi existencia.

salí de denver hacia el valle mágico (mas bien trágico),
en tejas . . . y mi raza es bella y hecha de bronce; soy
orgulloso y penumbroso viendo la confusa, la paradoja
de mi existir . . . marchas, gritos, protestas, demandas . . .

> ubicando mi mente
> es el grito de:
>   GRINGOS MATENLOS . . .
> eco de mi pasado
> y lo grité
> con furia y realidad
> corriendo por mis venas.

*llano as pronounced by a denver carnal

sitting here in my shorts, in magic valley court no. 2,
highway 83 east, pharr, tejas, i write in sketches the
never ending sensations of my life streaming in and out.
early today, a march in McAllen about and around the
need for chicanismo in the schools, and a chicanito was
dispossessed by the principal . . . a few weeks ago, ranted
and raved in denver, front of capitol bldg, read poem
(INDICT AMERIKA) and felt hollow yet real, fulfilled
and needy, and i made hectic love with my wife in
california street hotel in denver later than night . . .
still trying to bring about a redress for the emptiness
of prison (nine years of my life, and i am only 29 yrs
old); my new born daughter, Libertad-Yvonne, is now
gurgling out her need of my arms to embrace her . . . y la
adoro con todo el alma, she, born in northampton, Massachusetts, strange place for a chicano to be born in,
part of my escapade as staff writer/lectur-er for school
of education, u of mass at amherst . . . part of me died
there mid the vacuousness of new england.

> hijita linda,
>
> es bellísimo ser chicano,
> casado con chicana,
> tener hijos hechos
> del hierro de la raza
> de bronce . . .
>
> grito ¡VIVA AZTLÁN!
>
> siento orgullo
> en el pecho
> miro tu rostro
> y sé, vida mía,
> que embelleces mi existir.

the stream wends on and on and on . . . never a surcease,
tal es la vida.

b.s. ramblings . . .

an official kind of happening
where hunger and bullshit stalk,
riding on the emptiness of people
caught in the vacuousness of their lives;

siendo todavía cautivo y provocador
aún de mis llantos mas dolorosos,
i view paranoids running crazily
seeking refuge in embryonic arms

        like deluvial anger
        resonating hurt,
        deracinating selfness,
            spent like a used condom;

penumbra y desmadrazgo
derrotando vena y alma

sangrando,
llorando,
y gritando

        verbos angustiosos
        de mi santuario pasado
               y olvidado

made in japan hideousness,
recluse for a day,
fornicating
with kingly passion,
encloistered
    in thigh and juices—

refraction
        of yesterlethargy . . .

a jeweled escapement
en la gelatina vidal,
cauterized like burnt meat,
agglutinated
on the hollows of mine anger—

    a hard-on in perpetuity,
    stowaway on the last boat to insanity . . .

Juan,

works, words, numbers tumble down
        irrevocable happenstances in one's
                life

the cauterizing of all we deem to be our activism
        whilst we are straddled with bitching anger
        cum anxiety cum a million fluttering
                feelings
                playing
                footsie

with all that we fight   and we are sickened time after time
fighting what we view   destroyed, at times, by an
        unyielding society
        demanding that we conform
        to death
           in sick hues.

anger   angustia   angst   verboten monstrosities

INCULCATORS   FORNICATORS   DOMESTICATORS
                MAD*EEE*SON   AVENUE
                WALL STREET
         PENN*SYL*VA*NIA AVENUE

abodes for megalomania   creators of dementia praecox
        turning out schizos by the millions,
                long-haired, red-eyed
                  puffers
           engrifándose
                searching for nirvana
                    and
                      panacea,

finding recourse in irresponsibility,
irrational
       dysfunctional
            malfunctional
  hyper-paranoids swaying
  praying
      preying
         braying
             anti-self salivations.

                        THIS IS AMERIKA,
land of the pee-d off,
red for the blood-spawned genocide
        decimation of our people,
blue for the sorrow when we realize
        the cremation of our freedom,
white for the despots who have ruled us . . .
        AMERIKA   AMERIKA   AMERIKA

g-stringed, guitared blues, and funky thoughts
fulminations
steeped in our veins' wine,
drunk in callejon   and howard johnson eatery
                         regurgitated blood
    of our fathers,
      carving out freedom,
        patriotism rising like flag
        over viet nam
            like it did in san jacinto

holy holey wars   strafing our people down

the mass media like a mess   sung in holy requiem
a token attribution   in high C notes
denoting, connoting   far-fetched garrotting

        freedom lies
        sepulchred,
           buried
           in want-ads
alongside poster ad
    of zapata stealing watches
        (so the bastard gringos claim);

                    Elgin grown rich
                    on chicano carcass
                    and negro servitude

and the question raised
                              by white cupidity
                    is LAW & ORDER,
                                        damn morality . . .
law written to exterminate us,
order given to liquidate us,
                              and morality is 2nd best kept secret
                              in amerika,
                              chicano need is first!

frito bandito caricature
bandied about nomenclature
                              as if that were our nature
                              to be of comic stature
        just because the pinche gringo says so . . .

and our children read and listen
                    to power mad media
                    and they flinch
                              and sometimes capitulate

for they haven't the way to fight
      the ugly, rotten bastard might
of this canard, the u.s.a.

des-ma-dre   Desmadre   DESmadre   **DESMADRE**

and they strive
to un-root us,   cutting out our knowledge of our past
building gringo stories in our minds   from cradle to grave
as if we never did exist   outside the pale of their shadow;

                    but we are now arrived,
                    mentors to ourselves,
                    recalling mestizage past,

                    refurbishing our míctlas,
                    hispano/indios
                    proud and tall

like el pirámide del sol,
   the genesis of life
                     en todas las américas . . .

yes, we were the first
   and we shall be the last

                        for the granules of our tierra
                        are in our blood,
                        the air is ours,

                        and no s.o.b.ing want ad salesman
                        can take away our freedom . . .

we are free in soul—indian-spanish soul,
   like fire-passion beating the harmonic
                              music of mestizage . . .

we are mestizo   chicano

             THE BIRTH OF CHICANISMO,
                     born in fire and hurt,
                     living soul,
                     singing out our liberation

                     love personified,
                     we are the people of the sun

LA BELLA RAZA DE BRONCE . . . we are more than being,

                     we are past, present, and future

             HUMANITY ON THE MOVE . . .
                                 MENT.

migrant lament . . .

el cri-cri llanudo

canto y desmadre
among migrant deprivation;
schools filled
with tejanitos
fighting carnales
in ethnocentric heresy . . .

gringo asking
'bout right kind of chicanos—
people leaders
succumbing   to right answers . . .

migrant
tumbling offtowork,
saca llena de algodon,
from tejas to colorado,
michigan to oregón . . .

la raza hurt,
bent back—sacrificed
to gringoismo—
priests genuflecting
to pobreza,
lovers of destitution;

priests jiving la raza,
preaching
        LOVE THY MASTER
        OF THE BLUE-EYED HATRED;

a new age
has dawned,
            you, migrant hecho del duelo,
            scurry thru your work,
from grape boycott
to lettuce strike,
you laugh with new machismo.

91

migrant,
weep not over past desmadres,
pick up coraje y cojones
and
create
    una
        óbra social
               mundial . . .

Denver . . .

denver loneliness,
caught fragmented
neath neon anomie . . .
Chicanismo rapped en inglés,
tatteredly worn
como jorongo engarrado . . .

café   where
mexican hamburgers
are gurgled down
con cerveza y con furia;

crusade
        brimming
with cries of liberation
midst revolu-strewned rhetoric;
birthplace of neo-algo/rhythmic Aztlanísmo,
phenomenal crucible
bearing anger, hope and need—
tree shaded avenues
blanket-ting hollow-eyed children.

La Raza marches, chants, and hopes
hopes now lost
            in machination.

tomorrow's dust
will be as deadly
as pollutants
            now stifling our resolve . . .

denver,
bask amongst mountains
under el sol bronce de Aztlán,
trip on, eonized egoism, ramble
while la causa gains momentum . . .

someday
Aztlán concepts
shall become la realidad del norte . . .

someday,
        denver,
                someday . . .

preso político . . .

Chicano doing time,
being slaughtered . . .
condemned to serve
                    viviencia
fifteen-hundred years long;

it is absurd
to presuppose
that systems last that long;
long before your time
is served,
texas shall crumble
into
        the
            dust
as old rome did . . .

fifteen-hundred years—
years of cotton picking hurt,
years of burning deprivation—
eons killed by this damn nation . . .

and it churns,
on and on,
my being burns . . .

        bars criss-crossing
        convict minds,
        mente/alma
        caught in binds/chingao . . .

revolutionary, saint, or bastard,
feeling crunch
and fighting madness;
Chicano brother,
you are lost—
        political prisoner
        being defiled . . .

hung by balls,
hurt by hate—
little by little
you are dying,
day by day
you serve your time
only feeling emptiness . . .

emptiness . . . . emptiness
too damn eternalllll

y el alma muere   más y más.

motley

motley looking group
rapping health
        vis-a-vis racism—
sleepminded, anger oriented
        seeking la razón . . .

midst thoughts
    and genuflections
  spiced with mo(u)rning coffee
lamenting juventud
        angustiosa—

    todos gritadores:
                Nita,
                   Lupe,
                         Pancho,
               Antonio, Ron,
         Donna, John, Lucy,

los et céteras
    buscando
  documentación

del
    racísmo . . . .

aveces
i awaken
to a call
        stronger, carnales,
        than manic hunger or sexual lust

and it beckons me
onward   onward   onward
like a demon
rampaging in my soul

y pero
        y aúnque
                y además

i still fight
this demon bitch or maybe cabrona puta
ruffling, shuffling
my soulful yearnings

fling out, sing out,
string out, swing out,

a blaring, glaring madness
likened to a genuflection

and in this corner, they announced another pronunciamiento
testifying to the lack of testicles in amerika and only one
took exception—a very drunk eunuch on his way to a boda in
middle amerika where he was to lingually orificiate for the
benefit of bride (or groom?); just as his protest was to
break wind and waterfall, his misconception was abridged by
webster, who had a toxologist in tow, looking for a lex-
icographer to help them decipher

angry words

written in a restroom
by a demented veteran resting in ft. lyons, colorado, after
a siege by his love . . . and
the sad truth is
that love is often-times
worse than hate—for it can be more destructive
to minds already efficient in their dementation.

it was in . . .

It was in the year of my awakening—a social, sexual awakening that came about in Juárez. Ciudad Juárez, Chihuahua, México, that is. I was not less than twelve nor more than fourteen years old, when I first crossed the border with a couple of friends. We were not only young, but also a mean motley looking trio.

Three pachuquíos with burning eyes—coal black—ducktail haircuts, jitty kind of walk (hands swaying to the ritmo of our bodies, an almost sing song walk that kept our bodies attuned to our sing song speech), and the perceptible coraje that came from living en el barrio del diablo in east el paso. We were from the X-9 gang—batos muy locos, so we thought, and the switchblades in our pockets gave us both security and a throbbing itch to go out assailing a non-caring world, and thus by our strongly proving ourselves, we would be able to redeem ourselves.

Late fall weather was bristling about us, and though we had no coats or jackets on, we pretended not to feel the nip in the air. Eramos muy machos, and that being the case we would not allow our images to tarnish in the least. Around us people stared, for almost everyone had on a coat or jacket—while still the rest had on sweaters, and there we were: walking down El Paso Street toward the Santa Fé International Bridge, our light cotton shirts flapping in the autumnal wind— which had become rather brisk—and our long ducktailed hair becoming unruffled.

On tenement walls we could see scribbled down messages, as if they were talismans indited to providence—to a god who might care more than the suffering christ the catholic church had deigned to give chicanos: "El Heman del 2nd, con/safo 1952," "el alácra, 1953, c/s," "que chingue su madre el gringo—pero, en abonos y sin safo, hasta la eternidad." "Lalo el poéta trae los calzones rotos," "el focas del 7X, c/s," "SEFY del 9 del diablo, 1950, c/s . . . ."

I smiled at all the different bids for eternity and immortality made by unknown people of the night; pachucos, sensing the loss and hurt of their humble yet rebellious lives, striving to impress their names and histories on crumbling tenement walls, hoping against hope that somehow these same walls would last and become the eighth wonder of a society falling apart at the seams all around them. We walked on and on until we came to the bridge. Hesitantly we dug into our pockets and pulled out the required fee to cross the bridge—two cents each. Our pennies clanked down the coin box and we walked across as jauntily and cockily as possible, while inside we all felt ill at ease, though we tried to act nonchalantly . . . .

Early Friday night and Juárez was beginning to fill and expand; tourists flooded the streets—gringos looking for an easy lay at $3 to $15 for the night, and long legged gringas searching for an earthy, machistic mexican (a passionate spaniard cum latin lover cum fucking meskin) to give them the thrill of their lives—for after all, this was the land of super sexuality and total immorality. My eyes were taking in the hedonistic *élan vital* of Juárez—I was mesmerized and hypnotized by neon lights and blazing posters announcing and pictorializing the buxomy qualities of Torcha Flame with twin 44's (tits) or Ima Cocker, that beauteous blonde bitch from the old sod—a ge-nuuu-ine *belle exotique* from Erin, etc. My gonads kept driving my mind off cliff after cliff, as I eviscerated the lust/hunger of a child becoming aware of the scintillating allure of woman—any woman.

We turned at the first street beyond the bridge on Avenida Juárez; we walked a block over to Mariscál and walked down three blocks to a little club called the Chihuahua. I had often heard about this place. Mirna, one of the choicest putas in Juárez, worked there. She was already almost a legend on this part of the border. Every taxi driver in El Paso knew her—and I happened to have a first cousin who drove a hack for Yellow Cab out of El Paso, and he had filled my mind and soul with images of her; within me already existed an immeasurable hunger/need for her bartered caresses. No one was surprised to see us in that place, for at that time they would serve you whatever you wanted as long as you could reach the bar for what serviced you, as long as you could pay your way. We selected a booth and sat down to wait for the mesera to take our orders.

A young girl approached us—she was only about three-or-so-years older than me. Unblinkingly she took our orders. Not knowing much or anything about mixed drinks and having heard at some point about Scotch and soda, I asked in a rather feigned manner for a Scotch and soda, being sure to admonish the girl that I preferred coca cola with my Scotch. She merely shrugged in assent and proceeded to get our orders filled. Just after we had been served and had paid for the drinks, a slinky, well filled woman approached us. She asked us if we were buying, and, if so, would we buy her a drink.

104

We were so unaccustomly worldly, so sure of ourselves, that we gave her the once over in what we presumed was a man-of-the-world manner and droolingly nodded yes. She smiled at our callow youthfulness, turned to a couple of girls, and called them over. They joined us. The bargirl came over and set their drinks down. We each strove to outdo the others in paying for this tab, vainly trying to portion out bigger slices of manhood—desperate bids to prove that we were already man-size, not only in our minds, but in our ways.

The one with the piercing eyes and a soft curving roundness sat down next to me. She reached over and placed her hand on my leg and commenced rotating it over the joining of my thighs to my body. We exchanged names, and joyfully—nay, triumphally, I discovered that she was the legendary Mirna. The answer to my hungered prayers.

"Mirna, Mirna," I explosively burst out, "Cuanto cobras? How much for all night long?" My eyes, my very youth, my eagerness caught her fancy. She began toying with me. Her hands kept massaging me and I was being driven with the raging fury of demons burning me inside and out. I was febrile; I was raucous; I was blind youth! Andava caliente—¡Muy decioso, carnales!

What pleasure she got out of playing with me I'll never know. All I recall is that I felt like a man. Her hands crescendoed symphonically all over me—I shuddered to this long expected initiation to the realm of manhood. Her perfume was sticky and sweet, so sticky it was palpable. Her eyes seemed to penetrate, and her lipstick clung to me each time we kissed. She joked about robbing the cradle and teaching me how to be a man. And I? I was impatient to commence my education! Yet, I must admit that I was also leery in fear I might fail.

"If you are that impatient to become a man," she told me with a twitch to her voice, "let's get going." With that she took hold of my hand and let me down a long corridor. We stopped at the door, she knocked, and an old, fat woman opened it. I was confused, for I was expecting to go into a room with her, and here we were talking to another woman.

Mirna caught my confusion. She smiled, then she told me to pay my money to the lady, for she was the one who collected the money.

"Estás muy chico para andar visitando las putas, chamaco," the old lady laughed. "ójala y puedas cumplir con Mirna en la cama y no nomás con su pago." She continued laughing at me.

I felt mocked, but I wanted to prove that though I was young, I already had the makings of a man. "No nomás le podré complir a élla, pero también a ustéd si gusta," I responded. With that I reach down and grabbed myself, showing the woman the outline of my manhood. She merely nodded and smiled.

Then she surprised the hell out of me. "Take it out and let me inspect you," the woman told me.

"Why," I asked.

"I have to make sure that you do not have a sickness before you go to bed with one of my girls. I run a clean house here," she said.

Feeling a mixture of fear, embarrassment, shame, and queasiness, I complied. She held me and squeezed, then patting my testicles, she told Mirna, "He's big enough, now go see if he knows what to do with what he's got." With that, Mirna and I walked over to her room.

Once inside the room, Mirna mechanically undressed. I stood rock still watching. She saw me then walked over to me and helped me undress. I was nervous, very nervous. She reached for me and began kissing me. She motioned for me to return the kisses. I did. For a long time we explored each other's bodies—with tongue and lips, hands and finger tips. Then she slid under me and I needed no more coaxing. My animality exploded time after time til I was sapped. Still she persisted in more and more and more sex. Her knowing body, her caressing lips, her ravenous tongue, and her velvet fingers drove me til nothing more was possible. I was drowsy, almost asleep. She made me get up and dress. We walked out of her room. She went with me to the door of the club and handed me a slip of paper with her address on it. "Take a taxi there and wait for me," She said. "Later tonight we shall finish making a man out of you."

The process of making a man out of me was long and enjoyable. The last time Mirna and I worked on that project was when I turned 18, just a week before I joined the army . . . .

Recuerdo . . .

recuerdo un viejo fuerte,
con hombros anchos, alma llena,
y palabras que iluminaban mi vida

y tal hombre era
padre mío,
fuerte y cariñoso
como lamento cantado/llorado
ú consejo amoroso declamado . . .
hombre maduro y macho,
sin temor al mundo él vivía;
padre mío
puro hombre
un chicano orgulloso . . .
en aquellos tiempos . .
cuando
los militantes presentes
eran aún conservadores.
él ya era protestador . . .

east el paso lo respetaba,
barelas albuquérque lo conoció
en el nacimiento de este siglo,
        él entonces era asote,
        chicano que no se cuarteaba,

era Pedro Lucero Sánchez,
        su madre era Gurulé por apellido,
y él fué
        padre del barrio del diablo (en el paso);

era yonquero de los mejores,
        a nadie se le postraba,
su mundo lo admiraba . . .
        ese hombre fue mi padre

lo que hoy me puede, carnales,
es tristesa del corazón—
el día que lo entierraron
yo estava hundido en prisión . . . .

109

M. Acosta

months of blood,
year of hurt . . .

Chingaderismo . . .

the song comes on strong
        about revolú
                revolú
                    revolución

and all sing and rant and rave out   as if words could
                            bring about
                        change
                    while
                the world
            cringes in fear and more fear

and i hear un carnalito chanting

        "let me have a revolution,
            chicano power is my solution . . ."
        not knowing that absolution
        is not an ablution
of all the social ills
                    with their dementing connotations
            denoting kafkaesque idiocy
admist the hue and cry of zany librarians running amuck
        in their maidenform dreams
        about to rape the youth of the world
        with thigh oriented books
                            about sexy, whorey kooks
                giving kids dirty looks

in a world full of spooks, spooks, spooks
and all of them white, wearing polka-dotted jock straps
                in searing search for their lost or never-had manhood.
gringo te chingo
te chingo gringo
nursery-metered out angst
en el valle de tejas

                and i marched alongside
                    chicanos angered,

narciso alemán, lupe cásarez, lupe taméz, raudel, castro, efraín,
etc., and their words lashed out at an amerika called stupid
by lalo the poet,
an amerika i condemn and indict,
an amerika we all have come to be disgusted with . . . and if it
don't, yeah, if it don't change, we shall burn it to the ground.

allí, fuera de mi mente

out there,
where my mind seeks release
of itself,
where societal agglutination
becomes dementation

where birds chirp
outside prison cell window
in cold-blooded spasms
   of sadism-cum-masochism;

where
blood runs cold,
and confusion is the normal
state humanity lives in

                therein i shout
                my only protest
                to an unswerving
                monster called
                social obscurity

and i, too, hurt
unrelentingly
while lamenting
this dementing
chingaderismo

and left—far left kind of being left (out & behind)
with no choice (alternatives being parenthetical)
in the making of my destiny,
i boil inside
knowing full well the consequence
of inconsequential existence

and finally i dirge out my lungs
a requiem for a society now dying
and i know in the entraínas de mi conocer
that this society shall topple

even if it means my death.

Jacinto Treviño

bajo el cielo azul,
cerca las palmeras del valle,
allí mi alma brota flores
y mi mente ideas de Aztlán

Cerca de donde rinches
han matado y golpeado
chicano tras chicano
con gusto y alegría,

allí en el mero valle
donde está la cuna
del chicanismo
vive de nuevo lo cósmico de mi raza,

el coraje y el zumbir
de machismo y rigor
en el nombre de Jacinto Treviño
en un colegio netamente chicano.

Hoy canto canciones al viento,
escribo poémas del alma,
queriendo decir lo que siento,
mirando a un nuevo futuro.

Jacinto . . . Jacinto Treviño,
tu ideal mi mente habitó;
mi alma la angustia gritó
sintiendo la historia cambiar . . .

los versos que te he declamado,
con fuerza y mucho sentir, son
lo mismo que se ha declarado
al formarce un colegio chicano.

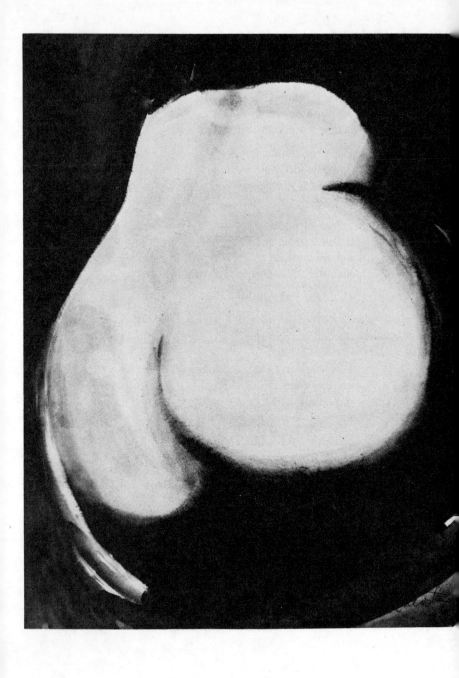

Mina o Quina

En aquel tiempo, carnales, yo era todavía un chavalón . . . un chavalón de muchos tanates. Era cuando los batos del diablo . . . ¿Eh, que dices? ———Pues, les quiero decir que los batos del barrio del diablo tenían una ganguita (una gavía, mas bien) que le habían llamado la ganga del nueve y ellos hacían sus cositas, aún ese tipo de juguetear con la vida como si fuese la vida nada mas que un chiste.

Yo correteaba por las calles del éste de El Paso, Tejas, y era uno de esos cabroncitos que nunca está satisfecho aún al no estár chingando con el prójimo . . . Pues, una noche típicamente Paseña, yo iba retorciendome por el barrio cuando un rivál de la calle Rivera se me puso enfrente.

"Oye, Juan Crujías," ese tipó me gritó, "me han dicho por hay que te la tiras de mucho arranque y que andas dando mamadas que tu eres el mero mero. Pues te quiero decir, buey, que yo soy el mero mero y que si te quieres aventar, pos aquí estoy pa'que te dejes caer, bato chapete . . ."

Esas palabras me encabronaron y tan mucho que pensaba que era, pues saqué el escupe—una pistolita que había construído de un pedazo de antena de carro—y me eche ensima del Chugatuerto, el bato mas desgraciado de todo el barrio de los Red Eagles. "Anda, hijo de tu madre desenraizada," le grité, "si aquí está tu mero padre, y cabrón que seré, pues ni a tí ni a nadie me le cuartéo." De tantos tiros que le tiré, y por suerte ni uno le fue a dar, mi sangre se apasionó. Y con mi pasión surgió un sabor de desmadrazgo que hasta mi alma se consumió. Renegué, grité, respingué, y hasta el cielo vi pintado con mi propria sangre.

Mientras yo resongaba, el Chugatuerto corría escamadamente pa'su barrio. Tan recio corría este sinverguenza, que hasta la calle rompía. Y yo, pues mas y mas me encojonaba. Como les dije anteriormente, yo era un pachuquío del X-9, una gavía de chamacos torpes y encabronados.

119

Al terminar mi uso de parque, me fuí andando casi como buscando mina de oro, pero mas bien en busca de los batos de la esquina. Allí en la mera esquina de las calles Hammett y Bush, cual hoy se llama Delta, me puse a chiflar y esperar. Poco rato después llegó una de las chavalonas que ahí se juntaban. Era una de esas chavitas pirujonas que capiaban con cualquier bato, y yo andando por las calienturas, le caí por un cachito. Esa chamaca que si era deaquella, pues se abajó con todo y nos aventamos los dos. Les quiero advirtir, carnalitos, que un cacho de cielo le arranqué y esto se los digo en caló y no en castellano . . . pues, lesvoy a toriquiar, loconotes, que esa chapeteada que dí, hasta la mente y el alma se me enrizaron.

La huiza estava, pero pa'que les cuento, a todo dar. Buenota, esa ruca, y con unos chamorros pero a toda madre y yo sentía una fiebre fuerte y chingona, y mis manos no cesaban de acariciarla. Hija de su, pero hasta san pinchis se me acercaba. Angustiosamente yo bebía de sus labios, me enloquecí, les digo, carnales, y sentía la fuente de esa chavita hirviendo bajo las caricias calientes de mis dedos, y que le pongo el parche frotado y me la llevo a un lado del canal y me pongo a quitarle la ropa, y ella pidiendome mas y mas, y yo con mis huevos hinchados y mi hombreduría lista para romperle sus ilusiones de cielo y miel, cuando siento un chingazo pero fuerte en la mejilla . . . y chingao, pero ese jodazo era fuerte y hasta varios dientes perdí, y al voltear a ver mi asaltador fijé ojo serio hacia el padre de la mozuela que en ese momento se encontraba casi desnuda—aún con la blusa quitada, la falda subida, el guardaceno desabrochado, y los calsoncitos por las rodillas. Mi mente protestaba la golpiza, pues yo no era el único que había hecho por conocer las carnitas de esa chica. El chiste mas popular tocante esa pachuquía era que élla tenía una mina peluda que aflojaba en la esquina, y toda la juventud le gritaba mina, mina te chingo en la esquina, y por corto le decían Mina o Quina, la puta Irlandesa. Peor que todo, traté de decirle eso mismo al padre de élla, y él con mas gusto hizo por matarme a puntapie y chingazo.

"Te casas con mi 'ja," me gritaba su padre, "o te mato aquí mero, hijo de tu chingadamadre. Me oístes, cabrón pachuquío?"

Entre medio de mi miedo de poder morir tan joven, pues les tengo que advertir, le contesté, aún humildemente, "Claro, señor Asote, que me casaré con su hija. Tan pronto como sea posible nos casaremos."

Nos casamos y durámos casados dos semanas. Una mañana muy temprano, me levanté y me fuí para siempre de mi pueblo querido. Ya tengo como veinte años fuera de El Paso, y en verdad, pero estoy ancioso de regresar. Mientras que viva ese desgraciado señor, yo nunca podré pisar mi tierra querida. Momento por momento, mi alma brota el suero de mi exilio . . . "¿Que dices, joven? ¿Que eres el hijo de Mina O'Quina? ¿Como? ¿Tú? ¿Mi'jo?" Sentí un latigazo romper mi corazón y en mi último momento de vida no supe si fue ataque de corazón o un plomazo de escupe. ¡Que chinga morir al no saber ni como ni cuando ni por qué!

To el Valemadre . . .

oye, tu con ojos hacia el cielo, el frío te covija
and it becomes you to lie in the sepulchre of your making
thinking, dreaming of panacea spelling it p-a-n-o-ch-a,
building nutritionless confectionary imagery to assuage

an empty soul . . .

re-cant trip
from juárez putísmo
to south el paso swollen belly,

and the streets
full of the semen of wasted moments
fill the gutters of your mind . . .

it is not a single individual
nor an oppressed group of people
who bear the onus of loss of dignity,

it is you, bureaucrat and politician,
ward heeler and power wielder
sitting on an ego-tripping throne.

you, indicted by ginsberg's howl, by gibran's the criminal,
by garcía-lorca, by azuela, by the hungry cry of a starving
infant . . .

sí, tú eres el valemadre y comes a costillas tísicas de los
casi-difuntados;

eres, sociedad vuelta suciedad, lo que orinan los perros,
eres el cenote atascado orando mientras que podridamènte
      oprimes,
eres el anti-humano que en los mercados gritas las grocerías
      de vende humanos . . .

te he visto
en mis momentos de desgracia
burlandote
            sobre mis desmadres;

123

he llorado   llorado el duelo humano   que aclara la
hermandad y tú   pues te has burlado . . .

hoy reconozco   lo humano que no eres tú

y por eso te rechazo
y juro que te quemaré, sociedad méndiga y déspota,
                hechizo de lo más podrido
                en la experiencia de la humanidad.

Let me . . .

wild bunch my illusions of a world caught in fantasy
and hurt; let me have a revolution, chicano power is
my solution; let me drive down the winding avenues
of my youth spent in el desmadre de zavala school in
east el paso, years spent in the unknowing of why
i hurt when

my visceral yearnings went beyond the sanitized madness of teachers, well meaning but racist, who could
only inflict their narrow points of view; and one of
them hated the thought that she could exist in time
with us, so

she circumvented her pent up witchery by bewildering
multitudes of chicanitos;

amidst the plastic hope of amerika fed on comic
book megalomania from
a mixed-up transvestite
called mary alias captain
marvel cum superman and
his sexually inverted
compadres—batsyman and robin—
to wonder woman and her
over-hormonized sisters

                    and the message was manna
                    about nirvana, and tarzan
                    swung in the jungle, from
                    tree to tree with apes of
                    all descriptions and
                    all the while he waited for
                    jane, white chick, to make it
                    to the jungle so he could rip
                    off a peice

125

meanwhile, tonto, playing idiot boy
to the lone ranger, would go into
town—get whipped and come running
begging lone ranger, boss white dude,
cat running show, to go into town
salvaging honor of dishonored savage

and out of the purple sage rode the cisco kid and his sidekick, el
mucho malo CRISCO KID, pancho, dripping mucho taco juice
and being mucho pendejo and time went on, no one protesting the
pandemonium in our children's minds, ad hoc committees were
never set up to deal with the psychic violence raping la inocencia
de la juventud until the 60's and 70's came tumultously around to
claim young mental tenacity and the world became a topsy-turvy
place and all of you old bastardos are the target for never having
the huevos to bring about change . . . some old fools demand respect, when they only deserve the emptiness they created.

c a n t o

oye,

    pimpo, talón,
    bato loco, cabrón

now
    reflejos de años pasados
    en el refuego juareño

imapout mymadness runtogether

night after night
hustling
looking for quick nirvanas . . .

avenida juárez
calle mariscál

        IMPALA CLUB, 1963,
        cuando la gente real
        espresaba víscera y entraínas
        i was jovencito yet
        bebiendo sauza con limón

        and

        tristemente sentía
        los trastornos
        of youth spent lost
        dentro refuego y desmadre

years have passed
multitudes have since
pressed down
my madnesses

new dimensions
come and go
like naked majas
seeking immortality
cloaked in immorality

mea culpa, mea culpa
o preacher-man,
gelatinous whippings
and globular sins

and the word emanates from the angustia y chingo, chingo, chingo
chingo, chingo, chingo, chingo . . . y me chingan todavía.

it is urgent
to re-cant
the question
of our human-ness;

it is basic
to our nature
to foliate   our sense of being;

life/force surging out
poetically blazing out
our societal-viewpoint activism;

knowing, feeling, being
human universality
cauterizing canto y llanto,
fortalizing humanity,

creating sensitivity
while charting
human courses . . .

> WHO ARE WE?
> we are the urgent voices
> venting expletives,
>
> praising our haunted sense
> stemming from our human-ness . . .
>
> WE ARE UNIVERSAL MAN,
> a spectral rivulet,
> multi-hued and beautiful—
>
> WE ARE LA RAZA
>
> the cradle of civilization
> the crucible of human-ness
> yesterday, today, & tomorrow
>
> MESTIZO HUMAN-NESS.

zumbido

contemplo el zumbido social,
encuentro mi llano almal
y siento el naufragio
hecho de ansiedad total . . .

        zumbido abriendo hambre tras hambre
        como relámpago furioso
        y grito el verbo vidal de amor
        aúnque mi mente no lo comprenda . . .

zumbido corretiando desafío,
soy todavía el desmadrazgo
de barrio penitencial,

        como proyección profética . . .

zumbido
      cantado,
      gritado,
      vidriado,
      vivido,
      enraviado,
      embarcado,
      sepultado,
      desgraciado,
oda
hacia lo desmadrado . . . .

the would-be gods

prisons create would-be gods—the type that become fortalized by
their ever expanding power to wreck havoc over powerless inmates.
yet, these same demogogues eviscerate fear whenever a variable comes
into their state ordained domain to challenge their quasi-deitical power.
sometimes even such a harmless thing as facial hair will be enough
to shatter their composure.

november 1, 1970, was a case in point. two prison captains and an
errand boy guard at one of the state prison farms in texas, went through
all kinds of changes . . . and i do mean CHANGES!

i had driven there in my normal, bearded way; in my pocket, i had
a letter from the warden confirming my "allowance" to visit my
brother.

i walked in through the front gate—an electronic monstrosity testifying to the utter failure of mankind to become humanistic. i went
directly to the visiting room, entered it, and stated my business there.
a guard took down the information. at the mention of my brother's
name, a prison guard captain stomped his tobacco chawing way over
to me. spittle clung from his jowls as he muttered:

"you all cain't come a-visiting here with all that there beard, you
hear?" his very stance was menacing. "ah jist cain't have you all
upsetting my convicts, and yore beeeard would shore do it. afore you
know it, all these convicts would want to grow one of them thangs,
and i jist cain't have it, hear?"

knowing that visiting regulations do not mention beards or the lack
of them, i demanded to speak with the warden. the captain directed
me to the warden's office. i walked over to the main office building.
an inmate let me in. a very broken shadow of a man, what with his
continuous "yes sirs and no sirs" to my questions. from the inside, a
horrendous voice lashed out to the inmate,

"boy, you all quit that infunnel haid-running, hear? i'll put yore ass
in the pisser, boy!"

whereupon the inmate subserviently uttered, "yassir, boss . . . ." and
went back to his tedious job of opening and closing doors and being
a whipping boy for the masters.

inside the office i was sternly informed that the warden was out.
meanwhile i kept thinking of the warden, realizing that this was the

notorious BEAR TRACK, a warden reputed far and wide for his brutal assaults on inmates. el oso, we chicanos called him, and i always laughed thinking that oso was the dimunitive of baboso. the errand boy guard called one of his masters. the captain came in and told me that he was going to call the warden about my request to see my brother. now, you must understand that my brother hadn't had a visit in over two years and that by institutional regulations he was allowed a visit every couple of weeks. my having a beard was not a violation of their rules, for prisons haven't the power to make the rules of conduct or dress for people not behind their bars. this was but another way for the captain to hurt my brother.

another captain walked in. he looked at me and immediately his nose flew up to the ceiling; he certainly disapproved of me. "you all come to see that boy?" he asked.

"i came to visit my brother," i told him, "and i shall see him one way or the other."

the first captain came over and spat out a message from his master, bear track:

"you all can visit for five minutes, hear? only for five minutes. you ought to be glad that we're giving you that much time. i talked with the warden and convinced him that boy needed a visit, he ain't had one for sech a long time." he stomped around, huffing and puffing out his beer belly, trying in vain to convince me that he too was a bad mother and that i better thank my lucky stars that i wasn't a convict. "now don't you all go asking for more; i went to a lot of trouble calling the warden . . ."

he realized the power he had over my brother. mad, despotic power over hundreds of convicts. he knew it and relished his hold over them.

my brother was brought in after having been forced to strip down naked. his eyes mirrored hope and joy at seeing me. he knew that something was amiss because we were having our visit in a room adjoining the warden's office. the hurt in his eyes was beyond definition when he learned that our visit was only for five minutes, instead of the two hours he was entitled to. he realized then that the state meant to destroy him—for he had become a thorn in the side of the captain's-beefy-excuse for-a-human-body. the warden was also trying to break him, my brother explained. it sounded un-real, until i began remembering the dismembering of convict minds by the brutal assaults on them by guards in the ramsey one prison farm. i knew how true it was, for i had gone through the same process only a couple of years before. there are no reformatories in texas, rather deformatories where human beings become mutilated vestiges of what they used to be.

the five minutes went by and we had to part. my brother went out to his cell block, to live a life that is akin to mental torture and physical abuse at the beck and call of a bunch of sadistic brutes in guard uniforms or warden positions.

i walked out the gate, turned and saw a prison official coming in. he reminded me of a well-groomed george lincoln rockwell, but with better manners and facades and an underline hatred for humankind. he was in his environment. he greeted the guard in the gun tower and asked what he would like to be doing on such a sunny day. the guard was taken aback and could only respond, "gee, cap'n sir, i surely doan know what all i'd like to be doing, sir."

i walked away feeling the hopeless emptiness of the place; knowing that the prison farm stood for the miserable failure of society to bolster the evolutionary process . . . that in order for man to achieve human-ness, prisons must be done away with, guards must cease to function as guards, that punishment can only create rancor. the answer, bear tracks of the world, is understanding and opportunity; love and care; and the strengthening of the individual. it is education and meaningful opportunities for creative experiences—not whips, guns, prisons, and deprivation. if civilization is to end and humanity to expire, it will have come about through the de-humanizing and destructive efforts of the bear tracks, captains, and guards of the deforming institutions that now control us.

smile out the revolú

smile out the revolú,
burn now your anguished hurt,

crush now our desecrators,
chingue su madre the u.s.a.

burn, cabrones enraviados,
burn las calles de amerika

> burn, burn, burn
> desde Wilshire a River Oaks,
> kern place to sutton place,
> burn, burn, burn

quemen la angustia social.

lift up your hollow eyes,
cast out your burnished hungers,
torch out your new resolve,
fling out desmadres viejos,
and burn
> the bastards down . . .

escuchen el canto nuevo,
sonrían la revolú,
que toquen tamboras fuertes,
y quemen ya la nación . . .

hoy broten
Aztlán de nuevo

hoy broten
la orden social

and burn out the old desmadre,

let freedom our lives create,
let justice our lives become.

los doldrums

post election
when patronismo retains
its choking hold
sobre   la humanidad;

cannon fodder people
work out
daily drudgery

politician megalo-maniacs prepare
the artful desecration
of all we term humanity

the day drolls on,
blasély walloping us
with random buffs & puffs

the day after
elections

and

no one
gives

a damn . . .

the 70's . . . años chicanos
Decade of La Raza

El año del chicano, 1970, came and went. No one was aware of it, other than a few of us. 1971, designated as many things is here . . . no one is aware of it either.

Let the world know that we are in the decade of the Chicano, that we, La Raza, have taken the entire decade to prove our case—whether in the courts or on the streets, but prove our case we shall.

Thus, in the decade of La Raza, we have started out with 1970, the Year of the Chicano; 1971, the year of carnalismo; 1972, the year of desmadrazgo; 1973, the year of retribution; 1974, the year of absolution; and so on, until we have taken our rights back, until we can walk these lands which are drenched with our blood, sweat, and labor.

Now, today, we call upon our brothers everywhere to join in this struggle. It is a struggle of the family; it is a struggle of brothers seeking to give birth to a meaningful social order, that we might all share and thrive together.

Understand, one and all, that the movement is not any one single color, but is rather a cosmic, universal man venture. The chicano is universal and cosmic—he contains in his being all the diverse races and bloods in the human race. It is not of white skin and blond hair that we write against, but rather the gringoistic experience that we deplore. The gringoistic experience must cease to exist—for we must all learn mutuality, otherwise, all this before us shall cease to exist.

The 70's thus mean much to us . . . they mean the fulcrum, the lever by which the world can change or be changed. The 70's are the signal for the impetus of the self-affirmation existential process to begin for La Raza. Those of you who are fearful of our self-affirmation, be aware that self-affirmation is also your right as a human being, as long as we do not trample each other in the process. We do not propose to be masters, nor shall we allow anyone else, irrespective of race and/or skin coloration, to be our masters. I shall just as soon struggle against a Chicano Caudillo as I will against the wallaces, rockwells, and other despots who in effect rule the world at this point. Despotism, racism, oppression, etc., have no fixed borders and/or coloration—but one reality we must all face is that we are faced by racism and oppression stemming out of the gringo community at this point. We must put a stop to this, and insure in the process that we shall never again allow racism and human/environment exploitation to thrive. The world and all its resources belong to all the people of the world, not to an elitist few. Thus the 70's must be the decade of cosmic man, the beginning of the merging of races into the bronze universality that we must attain.

EXISTIR ES . . . an experiment in writing
in and around a few songs
from the barrio . . .

From the glaze in my eyes, now stupified by last night's alcoholic residue, you might perceive that I am mad—which well I might be—but truth in this case is something else . . . you see, and this is a most emphatic and non-parenthetical thing, I am your product—alchemistry, alcohol, and all that crap tied up into a far from roseated package. ¿Y porqué te digo esto?

Muy simple—or may I phrase it precisely?

Allí . . . por aquella calle, en aquel barrio, existíamos. A fact, brother, just a pure fact. Unornamented. It was a not simple, yet not sophisticated way of life. It was merely existence to the nth power—y nosotros, well, we did love it—but not in the sense that carey mc-williams and stan steiner write that we loved it.

Still, I must admit that the same force and sense of life we had then has somehow remained with us. Chingao, pero nosotros todavía nos encontramos con las almas llenas de lumbre—and all that jive about some honkies having soul is nothing but jive. The Chicano soul is so strong that it can even thrive within prisons and poverty—while the europeo dies a horrid, wrenching kind of death. Empty bastardos, that's what they are . . .

But, perhaps, I should start at the beginning of my coming to awareness—awareness of my bronzeness, awareness of the uniformity of my unequivocable reality. Yes, I now fully affirm the fact of my being—and especially of my being Chicano!—but not too long ago I labored under the illusion that I was AMERIKAN. Came to find out that I was anything but that—and it seared me. For a long time, my space-time dimensional frame of reference was askew—past merged into present and future and I could not tell the difference between illusion, allusion, confusion, obtusion, and carnate reality. Even my tactility was awry. The entirety of the chicano mass consciousness became encapsulated into a single-purposed trajectory in my mind/soul.

In one of those turbulent dreams of mine, I heard a young voicelisp proclaiming a Chicano truism—"La música es como una mujer desnuda/corriendo loca por la noche pura"—and my very entrails

quavered with a love/lust that all but cauterized the veils separating my soul from my gonads. Even though at that miserable time I still subscribed to amerikanismo, the very foundation of my being jelled. Aprendí a gozar un poco más de mi Chicanismo, y me llené de furia encabronada. It was pernod and tequila coursing my labyrinthine totalidad—hyper sexuality and machistic self-affirmation. In one of the many granules that make up my existence, las voces del barrio sang of the tragic/love acceptances of life.

> los angelitos del cielo*
> le rezan a san andrés,
> en sus rezos éllos piden,
> por favor manda las tres;

puffy eyes and myriad minds, engulfed and struggling with mota and carga, lost—riata, higado seco, hijo de su—la vena llena and i feel spume fomenting like heroin trip, phantasmagoria and euphoria,

> los angelitos del cielo*
> se estremecían de risa,
> mirando al señor san pablo
> dandose las tres de grifa . . .

Frenesí came on rolling, strolling, cajoling. Impact compacted into duelo y canto; it was during one of these evening frenzies when I felt the realness of my schizophrenia . . . hijo de su, pero me pegó un chingazo muy fuerte, y nomás pude reculeárme, aún muy asombrado. Why? I questioned myself did I have to daily portray myself as a neo-gringo cuando mi realidad tenía mas sangre y pasión? Unconscionable delusions fostered within me by a mad, vicious society predicated on mendacity—little stings of awareness would now and then filter down. Those random self-perusals were cataclysmic.

I was jolted! Shit! I was more than jolted—estava tan encojonado que hasta mi alma gritaba con angustia. Chicano. Chicano! CHICANO! tales gritos correteaban dentro los laberintos de mi ser. Seguramente fuí acusado y condenado por sí mismo. Mi conciencia protestaba las estupideces clandestinas que habían derrotado mi pensar y sentir tantas veces, y yo nomás aspiraba con cada latigazo que resaltaba de mi mente/alma. Eres cobarde y hecho de mierda, tal mis

*Barrio songs by unknown authors (originated in El Paso barrios). "La Veinte y Una" (The 21st).

gemidos vociferaban. Aún yo me vinculaba aveces, con el alma queriendo dejar por mitigar las circunstancias—pero otras veces yo
rechazaba torpezas y demandaba de sí mismo que el fuego llanudo
de mi vivir brotara soluciones válidas.

Mientras yo pasaba por esos remolinos mentales/almales, la voz
angustiosa de mi juventud cantaba la absurdidad del barrio:

> queridos carnales,*
> vengo a torriquearles
> lo que me pasó
> en el chuco;
>
> salimos de juárez
> rumbo al paso tejas
> que era lo que
> yo quería;
>
> cruzando el rio,
> andabamos locos
> nos torció
> la pólicia;
>
> éramos pachucos,
> batos del refuego,
> chingones
> del east el chuco . . . .

Yes, it hurt. It hurt a hell of a lot to know me—my mind/soul still
have the scabs and scar tissue of nights spent sleepless and tossing
around; knowing the bitter taste of self-abnegation. No, don't look
away, you son-of-a-bitching thing, you taught me to hate myself. I
oftentimes get the same old urge to reach into my core and deracinate
that smirking/gloating me in there. Even when sometimes I lurch out
singing:

> yo soy chicano,**
> tengo color,
> americano
> pero con honor . . .

*"Queridos Carnales" (Beloved Brothers).
**"Yo Soy Chicano" (from the Movement: originated in Poor People's March).

My voice will lilt out self-acceptance, but my inner mind still fights me, and you dare question me about my societal decentralization. Of course, you funny bastard, I'm schizoid. How else could I survive in your cold, abject world? Your world built on equated hatred, premeditated oppression, and very methodical dehumanization. It was a metempirical farce. A gargantuan conundrum which was beyond the experiential hopes of any man. A horrendously circuitous form of anomie.

In . . . in . . . inwardly I searched, perusing every scrap of asininity that seeped out from my mind. My madness grew—a gagging-raged desmadrazgo took over; my reddened eyes purveyed a sick society gone over the brink into unsanity. Social impotence was my relegated reality, yet the need for fighting off your viciousness permeated body, mind and soul. You became the classic discord of the church and its proclamations—on one level the church becomes and is the people; on the real institutional level, the church is the clergy and the pope, and crap on the spectral masses that inhabit the earth. Shit, inhibit them for their own protection—world of derelicts. God of the wind and sun; god of gonads gone erotic; god of self-adamantation; god of womanbody; god of machismo; god of hembra; god of feeling—all you bastard gods now fully fucked and disenfranchised by gringolandia . . . in your places is jessie-the-kike-turned-european with golden curls and a penchant for sissiness. A mock commercial, bottled and labeled by the Reader's Digest, and shoved down our throats by monstrous mankind-hating conspirators like nixon, agnew, billy-the-kid-graham, popes and cardinals and nuns and true believers. sodium penthotal and dominus vobiscum with boruch elu haynu thrown in for economic luck. Oh, jessie-blue eyes, prey on my soul and castigate humanity, prayer to a preyer, and holy of holies . . . .

yo pensaba que esto era todo, por el momento—que nomás tenía que protestar y el mundo iba cambiar. Muy facilmente brotarían recursos—y todavía mas facil se convirtiería el racismo de los gringos a un poder humanístico. Sí, mi cobardía me enloqueció, y con todo el alma creí que nomás tenía que creer para que todo cambiara—¿pero creer en que? Todavía, sin darme cuenta, ¡pensaba como gringo, como déspota, como gachupín!

Once in what would be mere moments of my life, I would actually dare to just be. Oh, oh—delirium and all kinds of good stuff. I was! I existed in those rare moments without reason, without reservation—WHAT BEAT IN MY BEING WAS JUST THE FACT OF BEING! Mostly, though, I flitted back and forth, sometimes frothing at the mouth—other times disguised in do-good-ismo. My ranting attracted other ranters, and we became a mutual-we-adore-us clique. We had the rants down pat. We were in—so in that we most sight of the reality of our people. Hell, we had even lost sight of ourselves. We rapped about mercantile capitalism, its attendant hoopla horrors, the military-industrial complex (a crippling fixated need to bed down with unfettered militarists and industrialists!), the schizoid factorial in minority students, and a number of other topics—all predesigned to achieve a certain reponse from the college types we rapped at. We were los prestigiosos—los elitistas del movimiento—while los batos still had their lumbritas in the el paso eastside, their liras strumming, and their voices gemiendo:

> en el día siete de agosto*
> 'tavamos muy ahuitados,
> que nos sacaran del paso
> para kiansis mancornados . . .

Either we overaccented our voices while rapping and lecturing, or we became experts at gavacho modulation; inside the voice of the barrio growled:

> nos sacaron de la carcel*
> como a las seis de la noche,
> nos llevaron para el dipo,
> nos montaron en un coche;
>
> yo dirijo mi mirada*
> por todita la estación,
> a mi madre que la traígan
> que me de su bendición . . .

youth remained yet and i hunted down past. Circuity. Ever circuity. Never breaking cycle down. Thoughts gestated somedays. I continued onward in my quest on an off-and-on basis. Seeking blessings. I looked toward past, toward school authorities, and in return, they looked down at me. I looked inwardly—but i really hated being me, for my eyes were brown, my hair black, and my voice modulated sing-song accents

---

*"Contrabando del Paso" (an El Paso barrio song about prison and contraband smuggling, about sixty or more years old).

151

that did not meet the criteria set by a gringo society. It was still a topsy-turvy world. Surrealism and gothic inscriptions ran holocaustically through me—yesterday was the only dynamics for today and tomorrow—for I was born into the cauldron of self-hate. Viva la Causa I shouted in the vortex of my self-doubts, all the while knowing I had my self. Mesmerized by gringo mendacity and promises of crystal white xmas brought by a red-suited ancient hippie, I was paranoically confused. Oblivion loomed on the horizon as my only destination.

> ya comienza andar el tren,*
> ya repica su campana,
> le pregunto al mister hill
> que si vamos pa'luisiana;

and the train of my thoughts still rannnnnn on and on and on, with a sickly continuity; as if there were no punctuation marks to signal a respite. Though my mind said rest, my soul cried KEEP ON until all the gringos are dead—and my body, sapped of its strength, cried for a surcease. All the while, mockery stood in my way . . .

> mister hill con su ricita*
> me contesta "no, Señor,
> pasaremos por luisiana
> en camino a leavenworth . . ."

i was encloistered in a prison of inculcated hates; hates that reached out and in to kill me and mock me; hates designed to shred my humanity so that ameriKa could have shredded human-ness for breakfast—a blood pudding kind of feast, and i realized it not. Time frames exploded like expletives bent on carnage, and i came to for the nth time. Muerto sin saberlo, and refuge had stone walls, iron bars . . . refuge was grifa and mordant ideation leading to total self-abnegation. Brown . . . brown . . . brown, and the mirror shattered. I stared it down—it capitulated. Rant and rave, you bastard conscience . . . it is no joy being the sum and total of the Chicano experience . . . merged you are in the desmadrazgo of hispano father and indian mother, half-breed son-of-a-bitch whelping in your wilderness, with a cross for a banner and crujías for a crutch . . . there twixt el gran putísmo of life in the u.s.a. coalescing with desmadrazgo and espiritualísmo, and my manhood shrivels when i view my self-flagellation promenading like the great paradox, and sometimes my questions are

* Additional verses from "Contrabando del Paso."

rhetorically answered by patronísmo . . . and do i recoil? Once in a while.

> el hijo de la chingada
> es un bato que es muy loco,
> su vida muy desmadrada,
> del mundo le importa poco . . .

and though it mattered a lot, i grew to care less and less, and all the decals could only attest to the loss of mine own dignity. Once in a great long while, i would see Chicanísmo flowing and my heart would cry out need for carnalismo; mostly i would trick the world as much as i could. Hasta que mis manos se colmaron con la sangre de mi raza. Pistola desparando y filero ensartando, and i knew the cold reality of chingo . . . chingo . . . chingo y chingo más que al gringo. i was death and havoc cohabitating. Duelo angustioso deveramente haciendo por enyagár todas mis percepciones . . . yo era dinámica de la pinta—béstia sin corazón en los llanos societales.

> Contrabando es muy bonito,*
> se gana mucho dinero,
> pero la que más me puede,
> las penas de un prisionero . . .

i suffered the brunt of being a slave . . . of being powerless and stepped on, then i recovered part of my self—love and understanding and family,

> hay te dejo, madrecita,*
> un suspiro y un abrazo,
> aquí términa el corrido
> del contrabando del paso . . .

and even though time elapsed, and it hurts all the time . . . and i feel abjectness hurling down my way, aúnque "unos vienen con dos años, otros con un año un día, otros pa'dejar la vida en la penitenciaría,"* reconozco lo válido . . . and i lurch out again . . . caught in my own vortex this time . . . creating my own havocs and rejecting social edicts . . . it is no longer an equivocating i, but rather an adamant and affirmative I AM CHICANO . . . confused no longer . . . .

---

*Additional verses from "Contrabando del Paso."

Dichotomies . . .

So, lichen infested humanity, we have marched; we have fasted in our sanctimonious resting places; we have demanded, only to be reprimanded; we have smoked that last cigarette, then turned and demanded another; and now we again commence on that cycle of cycles, cresting on the tip of our crescents, bidding answers that are likened to crescendoes shattering harmony.

People viewing the universe with dual perspectives, and words somehow fumble out, tumble and pirouette on the hills, valleys, and plateaus of our minds . . . it is poetic, the merging of languages, thoughts, feelings, and observations so that one asks, "what time is it, carnal, for i have tantas cosas que hacer that it is espantoso at times," and we understand . . . and our ears reverberate.

People doing time in abominable prisons, being castigated for more than just breaking the law, and the rage seethes, but somehow the moment transcends existentiality, and an español flavored voice lilts out un llanto que hasta estremece the body, and shakily one floats on into the nether, vague, boundless, and jelly fibre one is deep down, where we find only more need and hunger. . . .

> now in the spirit,
> now in the hope,
> now in the love,
> now in the mania
> > of a people awakened,

> the sounds of a furious past
> assail mind/soul,
> ritmos y gritos

> tun-tun-pa,
> ca-tum-ba,
> tun-tun-pa,

> canto y grito mi liberación
> y lloro mis desmadrazgos,

                    carisma, carisma
                    tun-tun-pa,
                    i am serpent, i am man
                    ca-tum-ba, ca-tum-ba
                    tun-tun-pa

sounds of drum, sounds of heart beating, sounds of fear cascading, sounds of being . . . the trolley to júarez jam-packed, the women— tired, haggard—lift up their voices and give praise to the lord. A child, bright eyed and malnutritioned, sings for a dime. The day wears on, trolley crosses over to júarez . . . hot, sticky day. The old mercado, resplendant in the afternoon. Chile verde, tomate, uvas, cebolla, ajo, jalapeños, papaya, repollo, and herbs blind the eye and aromize the soul. Shouts leap into the air, "Chile a 4 por 1," "Yerba buena y manzanillo, queso y pollos," and we stop at the corner of 16 de Setiembre y Mariscal. We ask the man for ices—un helado de pistacho y nuez y la otra de vainilla. Eating the cones, we walk and walk—from the brothels to the cantinas, radios blare out on streets once dominated by revolutionaries the sad news that once again another, revolu- tion-minded líder had been killed in the hills of central México.

Cross the bridge back, el paso looms complacently on a sun-baked horizon. Buildings blot montañas out. It has changed, i hear a tourist say. Turn, look at him and laugh within. He sees my brown beret with Chicano Liberation button, and intensifies his peering. I peer back at the hoosier from the midwest, at his turista type serape and overly exaggerated sombrero. He asks, "What are you staring at?" I respond, "At your funny garb and hat." Ruffled and miffed, he stumbles away to someday brag about the militant he confronted on the International Bridge linking Júarez and El Paso. I continue walking, cross street after street, thinking and plotting a change of venue until the awesomeness of the El Paso County and City Jail is before me. Concrete walls and barred windows, I can see inmates inside shuffling time; I feel cold desperation; I am awakened to cold realities of having spent muted months, almost a year, awaiting indictment, trail, and castiga- tion—"perhaps we'll give you life or maybe even the electric chair, Sánchez," the d.a.'s assistant had repeatedly told me . . .

                    when was that?
                    years ago, ese,
                    when my wife with

swollen belly
awaited anxiously
her loved ones' releases,
one a son
the other a husband . . .

i linger
viewing mine prison,

inside i hear me chanting
canto y grito mi liberación
y lloro mis desmadrazgos . . .

liberated for that moment, then recall absurdity of mine liberation:
must report to the parole officer next day, fill out form and reveal life,
be absolved for the month, only to come back again and again for
more salvo-conducto benedictions . . .

just now had to bum 15 cents for bus across town . . . met some
carnales earlier who jived about famous writers and poets, they too
needed bread. They suggested i should work at UTEP, for poets belong
in universities, so they said . . . told them that most Chicano progres-
sive professionals did not think me qualified. "Por que?" they asked.
"No credentials, batos." and the movidas abound; other night, a sincere
gava bought me supper and asked me to intervene politically in his
campaign . . . wanted to crack the meskin community, for he was
sincere . . . took him for ride around my barrio—he saw our jacales
and was converted into a meskin lover; "Ricardo," he said, "I see your
realities more clearly now. I really feel that I belong, for I am sincere.
You won't find anyone more sincere that I am . . . etc."

ay, tonto,
let him liberate you;
his money can uplift
those haunted barrios
creating barriers in your mind;
he is good, ese,
he has prestige, ese,
he has power, ese,
he has amerika, ese,
he is mucho super amerika, ese.

let him hear
your tamboras
beating and beating
til his mind blows up
and his soul granulates
and he embraces
all those universes
you lurk in . . . ese,
ese tonto,
it cannot hurt all
not all that much,

for

seeing is believing,
you aren't selling out, ese,
just taking reparations . . .
so, pendejo, wake up
support him
just this once, then
después
you become huncho type . . .

no, i cannot support you, mr. lawyer turned politician. i, too, suffer conscience and reality. no, your job is meaningless; even now i must go and hustle bread and look at my carnales, those who do your bidding, with questions burning in my eyes. them i ask for work—those victims you've created. they know my need and hope better than you . . . their answer shall be a usual no, you have no credentials to work at UTEP . . . yet they shall continue teaching Chicanos about the Movement and use those things I've angrily written. we existing hopefuls shall duly create the BRONZE TORTILLA AWARD WITH BRONZE COJONCITOS hanging; we shall present these awards to professionals, bureaucrats, etc., for their unfailing presuppositions that they can arbitrarily define all needs.

persevere, bato, for it is perseverance and expectation to build, but not just for you—for all; it is your humanity demanding that you become strong and real, that you embrace even those who hurt you . . . build, cabrón, build, and lift up La Raza and all Humanity, and create out of your hurt and bitterness, forge out of your hope and love, and develop out of moot history a salient universe that is multi-hued and loving . . . it is understanding, not vicious backlash, that shall triumph.

> Chicano, Hispano,
> Migrante, Urbano,
> it does not matter,
> all the same,
> from vendido
> to regalado,
> from human being
> to human being . . .

> cosmic man,
> universal man,
> black, brown,
> white, red,
> yellow, and mestizo,

> all in the human process,
> evolving out of muck,

> turbulent, hating, hurting
> mankind on a rampage . . .

all victims victimizing each other; seeking an answer and respite for and from the basic insecurity of man—short span of life that goes puff before one knows . . . the enemy is fear, middle of the road squatting, indecision, ignorance, and clinging to a material world, when humanity is emotional, when humanity is intellectual—ay, pero, bato, you too cling . . . si, pues yo soy humanity, but usually on vacation.

> canto y grito mi liberación,
> también mi desesperación;
> canto y grito mi liberación,
> escondiendo mi frustración . . .

> la angustia yo les declamo
> y lloro mis desmadrazgos . . .

> canto y grito mi liberación,
> y vivo tal como puedo,
> buscando revolución
> jamás lloraré mi pasado . . .